The End

Published by 404 Ink Limited
www.404Ink.com
@404Ink

Please note: Some references include URLs which may change or become unavailable after publication of this book. All references within endnotes were accessible and accurate as of September 2021 but may experience link rot from there on in.

Editing: Heather McDaid
Typesetting: Laura Jones
Cover design: Luke Bird
Co-founders and publishers of 404 Ink: Heather McDaid & Laura Jones

Print ISBN: 978-1-912489-38-1
Ebook ISBN: 978-1-912489-39-8

Printed and bound in Great Britain by Clays Ltd, Elcograf S.p.A.

404 Ink acknowledges support for this title from Creative Scotland via the Crowdmatch initiative.

The End

Surviving the World Through Fictional Disasters

Katie Goh

Inklings

For my grandparents

Contents

Spoilers i
Content note iii

Introduction 1

Chapter 1:
The Pandemic Disaster 11

Chapter 2:
The Climate Disaster 25

Chapter 3:
The Extraterrestrial Disaster 45

Chapter 4:
The Social Disaster 63

Conclusion
After the Blast 81

References *89*
Acknowledgements *95*
About the Author *97*
About the Inklings series *99*

Spoilers

Plot points for books and films are discussed throughout *The End* so please note these chapters if you do not want any story potentially spoiled!

Chapter 1:

Contagion (film, 2011)
Severance – Ling Ma (book, 2018)
Dawn of the Dead (film, 1978)

Chapter 2:

Mad Max: Fury Road (film, 2015)
San Andreas (film, 2015)
The Day After Tomorrow (film, 2004)
The Drowned World – J.G. Ballard (book, 1962)
Annihilation – Jeff VanderMeer (book, 2014)

Chapter 3:

Armageddon (film, 1998)
War of the Worlds (film, 2005)
Melancholia (film, 2011)
Arrival (film, 2016)
Story of Your Life – Ted Chiang (short story, 2002)

Chapter 4:

The Handmaid's Tale – Margaret Atwood (book, 1985)
A Quiet Place (film, 2018)
Parable of the Sower – Octavia Butler (book, 1993)
Children of Men (film, 2006)
Children of Men – P.D. James (book, 1993)

Content Note

As comes with the territory of writing about fictional disasters and their real life impact, *The End* discusses a number of topics such as:

Abortion (pages 63, 64, 66, 78, 83)
Anxiety (page 56)
Depression (pages 54-58)
Infertility (page 75)
Miscarriage (page 64)
Racism (pages 14, 73, 74, 79, 83)
Rape/sexual assault (pages 64-66, 68, 69)
Suicide (mention of) (page 38)
Torture (page 66)

Introduction

The first time the world ended, I was six years old. People were partying like it was 1999 as news anchors and doomsayers prophesied whether or not a computer glitch would cause an apocalypse to herald in the new millennium. The problem – given the numeronym, Y2K (short for year 2000) – was that computer programs might not be able to read dates further than 1999. It was hypothesised that calendar time could roll backwards, like a taxi meter, to 1900, resulting in crashed planes, banking systems and electrical grids. A Y2K software outage had been deliberated as early as the 1950s, but largely ignored until 1999 arrived. Then mass hysteria broke out. Countries established Y2K task forces and fundamentalist religious leaders like televangelist Jerry Lamon Falwell Sr. decreed that a millennium apocalypse was "God's instrument to shake this nation, to humble this nation".[1] Some panicked, some found God, but most resigned themselves to destiny and kept partying. "What are we doing on New Years Eve? Well, I'm going to be hiding somewhere," Backstreet Boys member Nick Carter quipped nervously on MTV.[2]

It turns out the world didn't end on the first day of the year 2000. Computers ticked over into the new calendar year, elevators kept ascending and a pin was put in the apocalypse. I was too young to remember much of Y2K – my childhood New Year's Eves all blur together in my memory as a rush of my parents' friends' faces, fireworks and Christmas lights – but I can remember with crystalline clarity the next time the world ended.

Twelve years after Y2K, another apocalypse was foretold but, rather than technology, this Armageddon was ancient history. A New Age interpretation of a Mayan calendar that ended on 21 December 2012 marked the day the Earth would undergo a transformation which, depending on your doomsayer, could be a rapture, Earth colliding with a mythical planet called Nibiru, or freak weather. A minor eschatological conspiracy theory was whipped into a frenzy of apocalyptic prophesying by the internet, religious zealots and Hollywood (*2012*, the disaster movie starring John Cusack, was released in 2009). One in seven people were polled as believing the world would end on 21 December 2012[3] and I was, depending on the day, maybe one of them. A teenager with an overactive imagination, I scoffed at the idea in conversation and spent my nights reading blogs on the elaborate mathematics of Mayan calendars. On the date itself, I took some relief that mass catastrophe hadn't been reported by New Zealanders, who surely would have dipped into the apocalypse before the rest of the world, but I still waited up until midnight GMT, incessantly lighting up my Baby-G watch, before concluding that the end was, in fact, not nigh.

The next day NASA published an article, titled 'Why the World Didn't End',[4] explaining with the patience of a high school science teacher that the apocalypse can't just be speculated into existence by anxiety-ridden bloggers. Bit cowardly, I thought while reading it, waiting until the apocalypse *doesn't* happen to publish this.

In the long stream of history, Y2K and 2012 are hardly special occurrences. Look back ten years or a hundred or a thousand and you'll find the apocalypse. The end of the world has been happening, and subsequently *not* happening, since people could make shit up. Take the Bible, the original Reddit thread, which is riddled with Armageddon. Plagues, floods, serpents of fire and raining brimstone all feature as divine retribution in the Old and New Testaments, but it's the Book of Revelation, the Bible's concluding book, where things take an especially apocalyptic turn. Revelation's author, John, outlines both a literal and an allegorical vision of a future rapture, when God will make the world anew after servants of evil persecute the faithful. Four horsemen of the apocalypse, prophesises John, will bring disaster: plagues, famines and wars that will kill off a third of the world's population. When all hope seems lost, God's forces will return to destroy the evil and deliver a brave new world.

The Book of Revelation was written during a time of war and natural disaster: its author, John, is thought to have been a Jewish refugee who fled Jerusalem after an army of Romans decimated the city. Written sixty years after Jesus's death and a decade after the eruption of Mount Vesuvius, John lived in apocalyptic times. Revelation is a piece of political writing: a nightmarish howl for hope in a hopeless time. The Biblical book's narrative arc – disaster followed by redemption – has cemented itself as the prototypical narrative of disaster fiction and Revelation's legacy lives on as the most influential apocalyptic tale in Christian and, by extension, western culture. Two thousand years after it was written, John's archetype prevails in our fictitious visions of the end of the world. It's there in the technological anxieties of Victorian Britain's science fiction novelists, in the environmental disaster movies of the 2000s and in our 2012 (mis)interpretation of a Mayan calendar that followed the – then – worst recession since the 1970s.[5]

During times of social upheaval, apocalyptic tales and dystopian visions become manifestations of contemporary anxieties, from H.G. Wells's alien invasion tale of colonial guilt, *War of the Worlds*, to *Armageddon*'s pre-9/11 display of American bravado, to Suzanne Collins's widely popular *The Hunger Games* trilogy, published as masses of protestors took to the streets, demonstrating for civil rights, fairer economic structures and free speech across the world, in the USA, Hong Kong, Britain, India, Greece, Egypt, Libya and Ireland.

The end of the world as we imagine it has always been political, and intrinsically connected to the world in which we live in, because art has always been political. The popularity of Hollywood superhero movies after 9/11 has as much to do with American terrorism anxieties as it has with the average cinemagoer's love of big, loud explosions. These disaster narratives of paranoia, self-destruction and rebirth have always fascinated me. An overactive neurological chemical concoction of anxiety, depression and obsessiveness has led to a personal fixation with the end of the world, sparked as a child during a history class when I learned about the nuclear bombings of Hiroshima and Nagasaki, Japanese cities annihilated as collateral damage during World War II. The heinous ethics of that war crime resulted in years of being haunted by a recurring nightmare. In it, I'm forced to walk along a pavement for eternity, side-stepping cracks in the cement because, if I stand on them, I'll detonate a nuclear explosion. I would wake up coated in sweat after I stepped on one of those cracks, each a miniature abyss, racked with guilt at my compliance in the end of the world.

The word apocalypse has roots in ancient Greek, with *apo* ("off") and *kalýptein* ("cover") combining to form *apokálypsis*, meaning to uncover or reveal. The destructive connotations of apocalypse are more modern; in Middle English the word refers instead to a vision or hallucination. These two historic definitions – a vision that reveals – is why I believe we, collectively, are drawn to the apocalypse, in fiction and in the world around us. The end of the world is a wonderfully liberating narrative device and one that unites us all as a species. It's why storytellers, from Revelation's John to *Armageddon*'s director, Michael Bay, return to the end of the world time and time again. Whether it's a god's wrath, an asteroid coming to wipe out Earth or simply our own individual deaths, the apocalypse is a universal fear and fascination that transcends barriers of place, identity and time.

As destructive as the apocalypse is portrayed in movies, books and games, its original meaning implies an unveiling of the truth. It melts away the sheen of civilisation to expose our basest human nature and ask: what are we at our core? Disaster lays us – our identities, behaviours and priorities – bare. Boundaries are violated as an uncertain void in our future opens up. After the end of the world, everything is possible. We can be anything. We can be nothing.

While I have always been horrified and entertained by fictional disasters, in early 2020 this fascination began to almost presciently materialise outside of my imagination. A virus, COVID-19, spread across the world, turning into a pandemic and halting all global movement. As we locked ourselves inside our homes and watched as millions of people died, the gulf between reality and fiction became slippery. COVID-19 was unimaginable territory so, like many similar-minded people, I turned to entertainment to look for answers as to how this apocalypse might end. For a bleak few months, fictional disasters offered a perverse escapism. These stories had beginnings, middles and endings – they showed us what waited ahead in otherwise unknown territory. Apocalypse stories have always been popular because they allow us to live vicariously through characters – importantly survivors – who face terrible, life-altering catastrophes from the comfort of our sofas. They are small, contained apocalypses, Armageddons in bell jars that help us come to terms with the situations we find ourselves in. And what more distinct a catalyst to explore our obsession with the apocalypse, and what it can teach us about how we conceive of our place in the world, than the post-pandemic, post-apocalyptic future we face right now.

The End delves into the world of fictional disasters. It asks why we are fascinated by catastrophes as entertainment and what our favourite self-destructive fantasies reveal about our present-day ways of living. While it's natural to see the connections with the COVID-19 pandemic as we talk of contemporary catastrophic events – and we'll return to the pandemic as a stepping off point into disaster fiction – this is a fascination that has spanned history, across millennia, and one that is as equally influenced by the climate crisis, the realities of living under brutal political systems and the systematic oppression of historically marginalised populations. These metaphorical and very literal apocalypses are prevalent in fictional works of art, from pandemic fictions and environmental "cli-fi" movies, to extraterrestrial threats and total societal collapse. *The End* navigates these fictional realms in search of very real answers.

Art is a door, not a mirror. While there is absolutely grim pleasure to be had in pointing out the similarities between fictional viruses and real ones, these works of fiction offer us something more than just reflecting our current situation. "Survival is insufficient," is a repeated refrain in *Station Eleven*, Emily St. John Mandel's 2014 novel about a virus that wipes out 99% of Earth's population. The survivors in that novel band together as a Travelling Symphony, performing Shakespeare to the last people left on Earth. Even in an epidemic, even at the end of the world, art's purpose remains the same: to liberate, to connect, to propose an alternative way of seeing where we have been, where we are and where we could go.

Let's journey to the end.

Chapter 1
The Pandemic Disaster

It usually starts with a cough. Or shortness of breath. Then a fever rages, chronic fatigue sets in and muscles ache. In hours the body is incapacitated and, while some people recover from this stage, for others it's the beginning of the end. There's a sharp descent into hospitalisation as the lungs fail and the immune system breaks down. Death quickly becomes an inevitability.

This is the virus that spreads across the world in *Contagion*, Steven Soderbergh's film released in 2011. Named MEV-1, the virus is composed of pig and bat genetics, beginning in Hong Kong before spreading, on planes, ships and cars, through respiratory droplets and fomites – surfaces that have been contaminated. The MEV-1 pandemic is devastating. Early in the film, scientists project one in twelve of the world's population will be infected with a 25% mortality rate; by the end of the film, the death toll reaches 2.5 million in the USA and 26 million globally. MEV-1 is the virus that, in reality, scientists have promised for decades as new and old infections continue to emerge as a result of climate change and zoonotic spillover; the outbreak of deadly infection that will reverberate throughout the world. In short, a fictional version of COVID-19.

At the end of 2019, small clusters of outbreaks in the Chinese city of Wuhan were reported but mostly ignored by the general public. Flare ups of epidemics – Ebola, swine flu, measles, the annual common flu – are now a regular occurrence and, for those with access to vaccines and medical care, rarely more than a fleeting concern. But then the reach of a new coronavirus infection started to spread, moving through China to India to Italy to the UK to the USA. By spring of 2020, the world was in lockdown. Mass graves were dug as patients spilled out of hospitals and medical staff begged for more personal protective equipment on television, overwhelmed and not receiving the support they needed from their governments. The world braced against an unstoppable wave. The number of infected rose relentlessly. Global movement stopped, workers were sent home and mandatory lockdowns were implemented with the hope of slowing infection.

When you're stuck at home at the end of the world, what else is there to do but stream movies about the end of the world? *Contagion* became a lockdown sensation. According to its distributor Warner Brothers, Soderbergh's film was their most in demand movie of 2020, behind a particular wizarding series; for comparison, just a year before it had been the 270th most popular film.[1] *Contagion*'s viewers pointed out the striking parallels between MEV-1 and COVID-19. Both viruses hit the respiratory system hard with overlapping symptoms – a cough, high temperature, difficulty breathing, fatigue – and originate from a similar source, animal genetics, and place, East Asia. MEV-1 is a more fatal, faster affecting virus (in *Contagion*, patient zero, played by Gwyneth Paltrow, is dead within two days of infection), but during the first few months of COVID-19's relentless spread, when governments and scientists and all of us were trying to come to terms with the severity of the virus, its speed was like nothing anyone alive had experienced before.

Contagion changed from apocalyptic fantasising in 2011 to instruction manual in 2020. "Stop touching your face!" says Kate Winslet's virologist character in the film, echoing COVID-19 public health notices. Social distancing, travel bans and masks are implemented in the film. Soderbergh's camera lingers on contained surfaces; doorknobs, switches, handles have never looked so ominous. Other parts of the film now feel naive in retrospect, most obviously an absence of racism against East Asian people, something that sky-rocketed during the COVID-19 pandemic, normalised by fear-mongering media and politicians, including the then-president of the USA.[2] For the most part, however, *Contagion*'s plot runs unnervingly parallel to our reality, down to conspiracies running amok online, opportunists profiting off susceptible and scared people, and body bags running out. After Winslet's character dies from the virus, she's buried in a mass grave in a plastic bag, a scene that could be B-roll from a news crew covering the worst days of COVID-19 in China, Italy or the USA.

Another work of pandemic fiction that got a second wind during lockdown was Ling Ma's 2018 novel, *Severance*. As with *Contagion*, readers drew parallels between COVID-19 and the fungus virus that consumes *Severance*'s world, called Shen Fever. Originating from Shenzhen in China, Shen Fever turns its victims into a type of brain-dead zombie, condemned to repeat their habitual daily chores until they rot away. This is an apocalypse of the mundane: a housewife keeps serving dinner to her family; a worker numbly walks in and out of an office; a shopper keeps pacing around a deserted mall.

Other than sharing East Asia as a viral origin point, *Severance* is a very different apocalypse from *Contagion*. While Soderbergh plays out the cause and effect of a deadly, global epidemic like a scientist playing god in the lab, Ma uses a virus as a metaphor for the contagious reach of globalisation, the process by which the world has become increasingly interconnected through economic power structures and exchanges. *Severance*'s protagonist, Candace Chen, is a Chinese-American immigrant, millennial and orphan who works for a New York City publishing house, overseeing the manufacture of cheaply-made Bibles in Chinese factories. Her company exports their business to the country to keep costs low for American companies and consumers. When Shen Fever reaches America's east coast, Candace is offered a generous bonus to stay in the office while her company's managers flee the city. With no family to escape to – or for – Candace remains, continuing to commute to work every day. Unlike the sense of urgent emergency found in other pandemic stories like *Contagion* or *Station Eleven*, in which deadly viruses strike overnight, *Severance*'s apocalypse is so slow-moving that Candace doesn't even take notice when the city's transit infrastructure breaks down around her and the streets empty out. "I got up," she explains in the novel. "I went to work in the morning. I went home in the evening. I repeated the routine."

Severance is about creating a new normal in the face of horrifying disaster. Candace continues to work, just like how the people infected with Shen Fever continue to repeat their most mundane routines. As the novel's pandemic continues, Candace adapts her lifestyle until her life is turned upside down – yet she barely notices this change happening. We saw this very human ability to adapt oneself to external horrors laid bare during the COVID-19 pandemic as we, like Candace, adapted to a 'new normal' every day, whether that was clapping for NHS workers in the evening or wearing masks or no longer being able to hug our grandparents. Even when Candace is finally forced to leave New York City, she falls in with a group of survivors who organise their existence around repetitive scavenging trips to abandoned towns, a meticulously honed process that recalls the efficiency of the factory line.

It's hardly surprising that labour is the prioritised new normal in *Severance* and that Candace, her band of scavengers and the infected don't repeat other, more leisurely, parts of their daily routines, like watching television or going for jogs or spending time with friends. "It's easier to imagine the end of the world than the end of capitalism" – *Severance* is a testimony to this axiom, often attributed to Fredric Jameson and Slavoj Žižek. Capitalism, specifically late capitalism, is the economic system that has structured our politics, culture and social reality since the years following World War II. In *Capitalist Realism: Is There No Alternative?*, the writer Mark Fisher likens capitalism to "a pervasive atmosphere [...] a kind of invisible barrier constraining thought and action". Late capitalism is an advertisement, paid for by a cleaning supplies company, that eulogies office life during a pandemic. It's the doomsday bunkers being built in New Zealand by billionaires and it's the other billionaires taking off into space. It's the abyss between the richest and poorest people, the destruction of natural resources so stakeholders can make even more money and the privatisation of healthcare.

Late capitalism is also the conditions that make an office worker stay in her job during a pandemic while her bosses flee to their country homes. It's also the guilt Candace feels when she visits the factory in Shenzhen and sees the exploitation of low-paid workers who keep her employed. "It's just a job," Candace repeats to herself to quell her guilty conscience over the small role she plays in facilitating America's imperialistic capitalism, which exports labour to other countries with often horrifying factory working conditions. Late capitalism is how Shen Fever spreads in the novel: through shipping routes, a detail that parallels how COVID-19's initial spread can be mapped onto common trade routes, from China to Japan to Russia to Germany to the UK to the USA.

We are all complicit in unfair, unethical, unsustainable economic structures, proposes *Severance*, through its metaphors of pandemic contagion and zombie-like workers. Whether we are the business, the consumer or the office worker who files the paperwork, we are all part of a long factory line that exploits the most vulnerable to make a few rich people even more money.

During the COVID-19 pandemic, yawning economic inequalities became even more exacerbated as the pandemic saw the rich get richer and the poor get poorer. The global economy plunged into its greatest recession since World War II (in the UK, it hit its worst recession in 300 years),[3] unemployment numbers soared to almost double their pre-pandemic rate,[4] and many parents became unable to feed their children. Meanwhile the then-CEO of Amazon, Jeff Bezos, accumulated so much wealth during 2020 that even if he gave every Amazon employee a $105,000 bonus, he would still be as rich as he was pre-pandemic.[5] While middle-class office workers barricaded themselves into their homes, frontline healthcare workers, supermarket staff and delivery drivers and bikers still had to clock in.

In the first few weeks of March 2020, a shopping frenzy hit the UK. People panicked and started stockpiling. I let myself be buoyed along with the hysteria and went to my local supermarket to load up on non-perishables. Walking through the aisles was like an early flashback in a disaster movie: shelves lay bare, twitchy shoppers piled toilet roll into trolleys and nervous workers reassured that there would be more stock in by Monday. Rules limiting shoppers to two items per household had to be enforced. On a global scale, countries bid against each other for PPE equipment while suppliers reaped the profits. Later, as vaccine programmes began their roll outs, poorer countries had barely enough doses to vaccinate one in ten people against COVID-19 while rich nations have been accused of hoarding enough supplies to vaccinate their populations thrice over.[6]

Unexpected disasters have an incredible ability to expose capitalism's brutality, revealing in new light what is so often considered normal. It's why authors and filmmakers love to invent and use catastrophes – whether they're pandemics, earthquakes or dystopian revolutions – to push and pull at pre-existing ideologies and conditions that we experience every single day. In particular, the undead zombie has become culture's ubiquitous symbol for late capitalism. The zombie with its infectious bite and relentless hunger has become the perfect stand-in for the western consumer: never-satiated or happy with what we have, infected with a desire for more and more and more. Ma's novel *Severance* is just one of the latest works of fiction to use the mindless, chaotic creature as a metaphor for capitalism. There has been a long line of satirical, anti-capitalist zombie movies, the daddy of which is George Romero's *Dawn of the Dead.* In Romero's film, released in 1978, its four protagonists stumble into an abandoned shopping mall while fleeing zombie-ridden Philadelphia. The fully stocked complex is empty apart from a few zombies who wander the concourses. "Some kind of instinct. Memory… of what they used to do," explains one character, as to why the brain-dead have remained in the mall. "This was an important place in their lives."

The film's setting makes a clear analogy between the conscious-less, oblivious living dead and late 20th century American consumerism. The zombies blindly ravage without agenda or motivation, producing nothing of their own besides more zombies. In Romero's work, they are representative of the American consumer feeding off the rest of the world, a decaying flesh sack, stupefied and useless, eating for the sake of eating.

In *Dawn of the Dead*, the apocalypse is literally capitalism, as the never satiated zombies that pace the mall threaten to infect the living protagonists. They must ward off the undead or risk joining the horde of rotting, dazed and confused consumers. Barricading themselves in the mall, and killing off the remaining zombies, the film's heroes turn the shopping complex into a fortress. With nowhere to go – anything the quartet could ever need or want is stocked in the stores – our protagonists begin to consume the mall themselves. They ransack the expensive clothes shops, trying on whatever they want, posing in front of mirrors with guns and lipstick. The mall becomes a fantasy version of the characters' old lives, as they, creatures of habit, instinctively begin to imitate their 'normal' pre-apocalypse existence. Empty offices become apartments and are divided into 'family' units. Fran, who is pregnant, falls into the role of housewife as she and her boyfriend split off to form a nuclear family. Romero's film proposes that even at the end of the world, we can't escape what has been ingrained into us. At its core, *Dawn of the Dead*'s zombie fantasy is simply an exaggerated scenario of what we already are: unimaginative, powerless creatures of habit stuck living under uncompromising capitalism, unable to even imagine an alternative way of living.

Although zombies have been popular since Romero revitalised the genre forty years ago, over the last decade they have overrun culture, from television – *The Walking Dead*, which follows a misfit band of survivors in a zombie-inflicted world, lasted eleven seasons and was one of the most popular television shows of the last decade – to literary fiction – Pulitzer Prize winner Colson Whitehead's zombie novel *Zone One* was published in 2011, the same year *The Walking Dead* started airing. The hugely popular game *The Last of Us* – considered one of the greatest video games of all time – takes place in a world overrun with infectious 'clickers'. The South Korean film *Train to Busan*, released in 2016, became a global cult classic of the genre, while zombies have become staples of Hollywood blockbusters (*World War Z*, *Resident Evil*), comedies (*Zombieland*, *The Dead Don't Die*), musicals (*Anna and the Apocalypse*) and rom-coms (*Warm Bodies*).

Why the resurgence of zombies? In Ma's self-aware novel, a character called Bob, the leader of Candace's band of scavengers, reflects on the genre after another survivor mentions that their situation is like a movie. "Let's think about the zombie narrative," ponders Bob. "It's not about a specific villain. One zombie can be easily killed, but a hundred zombies is another issue. Only amassed do they really pose a threat. This narrative, then, is not about any individual entity, per se, but about an abstract force: the force of the mob, of mob mentality."

Or, the force of normality. Perhaps the recent popularity of the zombie movie is a response to how it feels to be in the early 2000s, living in a state of normalised catastrophe. The academic James Berger suggests that the recent popularity of zombies speaks to a collective cultural fantasy of violent social upheaval: "The zombie apocalypse is an occasion for imaging a condition of social chaos so radical that it sweeps even biology along with it."[7]

Maybe we are also drawn to stories like *Contagion*, *Severance* and *Dawn of the Dead* because they turn our very real, but often invisible, catastrophes inside out. Like stupefied frogs sitting in slowly boiling water, we adapt to disaster so well it becomes invisible to us. We have been living under the slow-burning consequences of western capitalism's relentless, violent expansion for centuries but only when a disaster suddenly becomes urgent, like a pandemic, do we sit up and take notice. COVID-19 simply exacerbated what we, as a society, already know and seemingly accept: that some lives are deemed more important than others; that the accumulation of capital wealth is more valuable than workers' safety; that even a pandemic couldn't slow the wheels of capital gain.

During the COVID-19 pandemic, anxieties around contagion, infection and crowded spaces became part of our traumatised zeitgeist, and pandemic stories – whether eerily realistic, like *Contagion*, or undead fantasies, like *Dawn of the Dead* – offered comfort in their three-act structures, ridiculous plots and surviving-against-the-odds characters. But fictional hordes of zombies, decimated cities and deadly viruses can also encapsulate how it feels to live in a time of looming disaster, whether that's a pandemic, the climate crisis or living under the unsustainable, unbearable freefall of late capitalism. As we watch survivors try to band together and thrive in their post-apocalyptic worlds, maybe we're not watching *what if?* hypothesised visions of our future. Maybe *Contagion*'s pandemic and *Serverance*'s work-aholic infected tell us more about how we were living before COVID-19, before we started looking to films and books to tell us how a real pandemic might play out. Maybe these stories tell us more about how we have always lived and how we will continue to live as we stumble forward, feeding off other countries and other people, consuming our own planet without thought, living as if we were zombies, severed from each other and our collective humanity.

Chapter 2
The Climate Disaster

Dolphins, announced the internet, were returning to Venice's canals. So were swans. Elephants were wandering through Chinese villages and deer through American metropolitans. People in cities reported hearing more birdsong than normal, seeing more butterflies and bees. Did the air smell fresher? Was the grass in the park a little greener? The sky a little bluer?

"Nature is healing, *we* are the virus," people wrote in Instagram captions and tweets alongside photos of happy, roaming animals. The sincerity of these "nature is healing" social media posts peaked in March 2020, and although they inevitably mocked as memes, these photos offered slivers of a silver lining as we doomscrolled online during what felt like the end of the world.

While many of those animal photos were debunked as fake – dolphins were, unfortunately, not swimming down Venice's canals – there was, tied into this, a genuine hope that the one up-side to a global lockdown would be reduced levels of pollution, and a demonstrable impact on the environment. As fleets of airplanes sat landbound in airports and cars disappeared from motorways, some theorised and hoped that this would be a turning point for the climate crisis we are currently living in.

A few months before doctored animal photos went viral, we rang in the third decade of the new millennium and life on Earth resembled a dystopian simulation. In Australia, bushfires raged, decimating land and killing over one billion animals,[1] while the sea – growing more acidic by the minute – continued to bleach the Great Barrier Reef. Droughts, now in their second, third or fourth year, continued to bring famine to Zambia, Ethiopia, Sudan and Chad. From Mumbai to Wuhan, London to Los Angeles, air pollution choked cities, wetlands disappeared and deserts expanded. Heatwaves broke records. In the summer of 2021, the UK's Met Office issued its first ever extreme heat warning as roads melted, and Northern Ireland recorded its highest temperature on record.[2]

To say that life on Earth is becoming unmanageable is an understatement. During heatwaves, it's become common for people to tweet, "this is just trying to commute during the climate crisis," accompanied by stills from *Mad Max: Fury Road* – George Miller's 2015 dystopian film about a society without water – that shows characters manically driving through the desert. Jokes aside, as we inch closer to the deadline marking when the climate crisis will no longer be reversible, real life is beginning to share startling similarities with Miller's post-apocalyptic nightmare.

The first *Mad Max* film was released in 1979 and stars Mel Gibson as Max, a police officer who is tasked with enforcing the law in a lawless future society. In the film, gangs battle over oil – a detail that mirrors the real oil shortages of 1979, an energy crisis that followed the Iranian Revolution. In *Mad Max*, chaos reigns, but it doesn't come close to the barren wasteland of *Mad Max: Fury Road*, released forty years after the original. In *Fury Road*, Max, now a PTSD-stricken, mute anti-hero, is recast as Tom Hardy and the oil energy crisis is replaced with an even more deficient and vital resource – water. A cruel overlord called Immortan Joe, controls the land's last water supply and uses brainwashed orphan boys to do his bidding. Locked within his Citadel are a group of young women, Immortan Joe's 'wives' who are little more than breeding stock to the autocrat.

In *Fury Road*'s parched kingdom, Immortan Joe casts himself as a god, radicalising young men and controlling women's bodies. The water crisis is the source of his power and this apocalyptic concoction of toxic masculinity, a freak climate and limited resources controlled by the tyrannical few, casts a nightmarish vision of a future that contains more than a few shades of our real, present-day world.

"Humanity is waging war on nature," said António Guterres, secretary general of the United Nations, in a sombre, end-of-2020 speech titled 'The State of the Planet' at Columbia University in New York.[3] "This is suicidal," he continued. "Biodiversity is collapsing. One million species are at risk of extinction. Ecosystems are disappearing before our eyes." Nine million people died from air pollution in 2020.[4] Seven million people died from hunger, directly and indirectly caused by climate change.[5] Based on current emissions, we have until 2027 before we cross the threshold for disastrous, irreversible global warming.

Catastrophic visions of the future, like *Fury Road*'s, look less fictional and more prescient with every passing year. For a long time, the climate crisis felt like a slow-burning apocalypse. Something for the next generation, and the generation after that, and the generation after that to worry about. Sure, freak weather, earthquakes and heatwaves are becoming the norm but we've got at least fifty years to sort it out. Then it was thirty years. Then fifteen. Maybe ten. Now… As you read this, who can say how many. For scientists, the climate crisis has accelerated at a rate comparable to a rampant epidemic but for older generations it crept up before, suddenly, it was everywhere. For my generation, who sat down to watch *An Inconvenient Truth* – the Al Gore-starring, Oscar-winning climate documentary – in biology class, we grew up with an acute awareness that we are living in the sixth mass extinction. The climate crisis has been a never-ending apocalypse, chugging along since before many of us were even born.

Images of polar bears marooned on ice caps, fires raging and seas shrinking have become teatime viewing. In the west there is a sense that climate change is something happening *over there*, as if over there was on a different planet and not intertwined with each individual life on Earth. Climate change has become so normalised, it is almost mundane. Coupled with the perception that it is also something foreign – and therefore removed from the everyday lives of those in the Global North who live in relatively mild climates – the Earth's sixth mass extinction has assimilated into our banal, everyday lives.

While horrifying, this isn't especially surprisingly. History has shown us, time and time again, that people acclimatise to even the most abominable circumstances; every nation has lived with war, genocide and brutal regimes as victim and perpetrator. The truth is, it is far too easy to live with the climate crisis as it is right now, if you live in a place safe from its most damaging impacts, removed from the suffering it is already causing in other regions. That isn't to say that people are apathetic about our world's environmental disaster. Walk up to the average stranger on the street, ask them if the climate crisis is a concern, and more times than less, they'll respond with a resounding yes. A 2019 poll revealed that 85% of British people are concerned about climate change and 73% believe we are already feeling its impact.[6]

Living with the knowledge of the climate crisis is living between two poles: the numbness of normalisation and the paralysis of existential helplessness. It is exhausting. It's also important to note that this fatigue at the prospect of an impending mass extinction is less to do with our species' callousness, and more directly connected with political helplessness and dogged capitalism. How can one person stop the flood that is coming when our political leaders are more concerned with corporations' interests than the wellbeing of their own people? How can we – as individuals – turn the tides on a looming catastrophe that might wipe out life as we know it?

The psychological reality of living with these two combating states of emotional extremity is what Susan Sontag contemplates in 'The Imagination of Disaster'. In this 1965 essay, she writes, "We live under continual threat of two equally fearful, but seemingly opposed, destinies: unremitting banality and inconceivable terror."[7] Sontag was not writing about the climate crisis, but rather the sociopolitical crises of the 1950s and '60s – predominately the Cold War. Fantasy, she decides in the essay, is what helps us cope with these two forces of banality and terror, specifically popular science fiction movies from that time, like *Godzilla* and *The Invasion of the Body Snatchers*. Like how fictional pandemics offered a perverse catharsis to audiences during the COVID-19 pandemic, the popularity of these sci-fi movies worked to numb and dissipate nuclear fears of the McCarthy era. Familiar narrative arcs and the normalisation of what is psychologically unbearable creates an apathy in the audience, argues Sontag. "We are merely spectators; we watch." Political helplessness is transposed into the movie-going experience.

Our present-day natural disaster movies do to the climate crisis what Sontag's sci-fi disasters did to nuclear fears. The Hollywood blockbuster *San Andreas* (2015) dramatises an imaginary 'Big One' earthquake, which in reality is long overdue along the San Andreas fault line – where two tectonic plates meet – in California. The film's structure is conventional for Hollywood disaster movies. Our hero (Dwayne 'The Rock' Johnson) is a firefighter, prepared for earthquakes with convenient access to a helicopter. When the 'Big One' begins, he must bring his separated family together during the disaster, while bespectacled scientists, who have predicted the magnitude of the earthquake, struggle to get the word out to the public. Mass destruction ensues, including the demise of L.A. and San Francisco. Tidal waves crash across the Golden Gate Bridge, buildings are torn apart like toys and fissions rip apart freeways – all of which is observed by Johnson and his family flying high above the carnage in their helicopter. *San Andreas* is, as most disaster movies are, told through the eyes of one family who are reconciled by the trauma of surviving the end of the world. Johnson's character and his wife's impending divorce is portrayed as being as apocalyptic for them as the destruction of California is for its citizens. A supersized earthquake is made manageable by this storytelling, a natural disaster turned into context for a family's strife. Watching with the knowledge that this is a Hollywood movie with Johnson at its wheel, we know that a happy ending is as inevitable as a 'Big One' earthquake is for California.

Another freak environmental movie, *The Day After Tomorrow* (2004) similarly turns a disaster into an inciting incident for a family's domestic troubles. In the film, climatologist Jack (Dennis Quaid) predicts that climate change will disrupt the Atlantic Meridional Overturning Circulation – an ocean current that mediates eastern America and western Europe's climates – bringing about a new ice age. Despite warning world leaders, Jack's data is dismissed by the American Vice President who tells him, "Our economy is every bit as fragile as the environment."

In the film, birds depart south at double speed, snow begins to fall in New Delhi and freak turbulence nearly brings planes down, including the plane of Jack's son, Sam, who is on his way to New York City for an academic decathlon tournament. Overnight, a polar vortex engulfs the world, turning America's east coast into an Arctic landscape and Jack must trek from Washington, D.C. to New York to rescue his son.

The Day After Tomorrow is a very silly film and one that I love. Most of its tension comes from Jack's journey through blizzards and Sam's many near-death escapades in a frozen New York City. Why exactly is Sam abandoning his scientific research that could save millions to walk thousands of miles to look for his son who may or may not be dead? Seemingly, he feels like he needs to make it up to his son for neglecting him in favour of his climatology research. Nothing makes sense and it doesn't really need to. The ice age is merely the setting against which the father-son drama plays out. Of course, Jack and Sam are reconciled and the film ends on an optimist note with climate refugees moving south across the Mexican border. The resolution is comforting: sure, an ice age might kill off millions and decimate our climate, but at least some of us will survive. We'll get through it.

The Day After Tomorrow and *San Andreas* are part of a recent storytelling genre dubbed climate fiction, or cli-fi. These climate disaster movies are predictable – in premise, narrative and ending – following an arc that is natural to Hollywood but very unnatural to real life. On screen, natural disasters are arranged into neat three-act structures, typically with happy endings for their protagonist heroes. In reality, the climate crisis is a sprawling, ugly tale. It begins and ends relentlessly. The bushfires raging in Australia, the famines that killed thousands in Madagascar, Ethiopia and Haiti, the 4,000-year-old Canadian ice shelf (the country's last) that calved into the sea[8] – all of these climate-related cataclysm events from very recent memory are side effects of the crisis that has engulfed our planet. Our brains cannot fathom these losses. We can barely conceive of the enormity and gravity of the climate crisis and these movies, through their narrow character-driven lenses, circumvent the big picture into something more easy to process: a loss, a reunion, a sliver of survival, a happy ending.

"The climate crisis is also a crisis of culture, and thus of the imagination," writes Amitav Ghosh in his book *The Great Derangement.*[9] Culture, argues Ghosh, has no idea how to cope with climate disaster. It rarely appears in our fiction and, when it does, it is relegated to sci-fi, speculative fiction and fantasy. We need a new language for the climate crisis, one that doesn't sever it from real life consequences or treat it as backdrop. It feels, frankly, perverse that we feel more emotionally entangled in the stakes of one fictional nuclear family than in the lives of millions of climate refugees – and yet, who can blame us when our real life climate disasters leave us feeling so helpless.

As the most pressing current concern facing our planet, what are the ethics of movies, like *San Andreas*, *The Day After Tomorrow* and many others, that use the climate crisis as context for character development? Do they bring new light and human interest to natural disasters or do they contribute to our inherent failure to understand the climate crisis beyond happy endings and shock value?

I don't believe that disaster movie filmmakers should be used as scapegoats for the climate crisis when governments and corporations, bodies that can implement the necessary changes to hinder real environmental disaster, refuse to act. Art should not be treated like policy, and I don't believe that anyone seriously expects Hollywood blockbusters to be the main tools we use to educate people about the climate crisis. These films are simply part of a larger cultural failure to tackle the debilitating magnitude of the stakes of disaster; their biggest crime, a lack of imagination. Hollywood's cli-fi movies have barely progressed past Biblical archetypes in which God's wrath annihilates human ego, sinners are condemned to death and the righteous are saved.

Human interest does not have to be sacrificed in order to tell a more 'authentic' story of the climate crisis either.

There has never been a calamity that has demanded more human interest than environmental disaster, and investing emotional stakes into the climate crisis is something fiction *can* do. A novel, like Jenny Offill's *Weather* (2020), can capture our fragmented, overwhelmed, dismayed brains during the climate crisis. "First, they came for the coral, but I did not say anything because I was not a coral," thinks *Weather*'s protagonist. Another 2020 novel, Lydia Millet's *A Children's Bible*, can demonstrate environmentalism's generational strife through blistering allegory, as a group of children are left to look after their parents when a storm hits their holiday house.

While Hollywood cli-fi blockbusters tend to locate their action in an overnight change – suddenly, an ice age; suddenly, an earthquake – other speculative fiction moves the action to the post-apocalyptic fallout of a post-environmental crisis. The British writer J.G. Ballard is frequently called the great climate crisis foreshadower; his books *The Drowned World* (1962) and *The Drought* (1965), in which the planet is transformed by man-made environmental disaster, are increasingly being reevaluated as realist novels rather than science fiction.

"Soon it would be too hot," reads the line that opens *The Drowned World*. In the novel, the temperature at the Equator has risen to 180 degrees and the melted polar caps have flooded the world. The Earth's population (a cool five million) has moved to the Arctic and Antarctic Circles.

Europe is a series of lagoons and London is a submerged, stifling tropic wilderness. Mosquitoes are the size of dragonflies, iguanas and wolf spiders hide in the shadows, and flora and fauna from the Triassic period flourish.

The novel's protagonist, Kerans, is part of a surveyor team sent to test whether Europe could ever become habitable again. In this strange, prehistoric climate, the team becomes psychologically affected. Rather than sleep, Kerans experiences 'time jungles', made up of 'archaic memories' as he drifts back into a prehistoric mentality. "Guided by his dreams, he was moving backwards through the emergent past, through a succession of ever stranger landscapes, centred upon the lagoon."

Ballard was born in Japanese-occupied Shanghai and spent three years in an internment camp as a child. His fiction is haunted by themes of social de-evolution and regression, inspired by his early wartime experiences. "The realities that you took for granted – the comfortable day-to-day life, school, the home where one lives [...] were just a stage set," said Ballard in conversation with Travis Elborough for *The Drowned World*'s afterword. "They could be dismantled overnight." The novel uses an ecological crisis to shatter the illusion of civilisation. Kerans 'de-evolves' through the novel until he no longer sees purpose in searching for humanity's future through his research. At the end of the novel, he abandons his colleagues to venture south to the novel's heart of darkness, an uninhabitable Equator – "a second Adam searching for the forgotten paradises of the reborn sun."

Mapping the effects of climate change onto our psyche also lies at the heart of Jeff VanderMeer's Southern Reach trilogy, which begins with *Annihilation* (2014). The novel's unnamed protagonist, a biologist who has recently lost her husband, narrates the events of an expedition into Area X, a mysterious, untouched climate that has emerged along the USA's coastline after an 'Event'. Area X's creatures and foliage are mutations and the place has been abandoned by its former human inhabitants although remnants – a village, a lighthouse, a tower – remain. Into this Edenic wilderness goes the biologist's expedition, the twelfth of its kind to be sent by the governmental body, Southern Reach, who are no closer to solving what exactly Area X is. Along with the biologist goes an anthropologist, a psychologist and a surveyor – an all-women team, the only controlled variant in Southern Reach's experimental excursion.

The biologist's expedition is doomed from its inception, like those that went before it: the second expedition committed suicide, the third killed each other and the eleventh returned, but with their former selves scraped out, their bodies soon rotting from contamination. Annihilation is an inevitability, not a possibility, in Area X. So, why go on this self-destructive expedition? Slowly the biologist reveals that her husband was part of the eleventh expedition that returned home from Area X as ghosts of their former selves. Rather than scientific enquiry, the biologist has volunteered to go into Area X to find out what her husband encountered there. Grief, then, is her motivation.

The inspiration for Area X came from the Deepwater Horizon oil spill that discharged 4.9 million barrels of oil into the Gulf of Mexico. "We didn't know if it would ever end," VanderMeer told *The Atlantic* about the disaster.[10] "Some experts were saying there might still be oil spilling in twenty years from now. There was a constant spillage in your head. A constant drip in your head." Like Ballard's *The Drowned World*, Area X's climate is an uncanny manifestation of the natural world, one that is both futuristic and prehistoric. Its environment is constantly transforming, from beach to swamp to forest. And rather than toxic, it is pristine: "The air was so clean, so fresh, while the world back beyond the border was what it had always been during the modern era: dirty, tired, imperfect, winding down, at war with itself." In Alex Garland's 2017 film adaptation of *Annihilation*, the ever-expanding border around Area X is a vertical oil spill, a slick, swirling rainbow of toxins trapped outside the immaculate nature.

"The beauty of [it] cannot be understood, either, and when you see beauty in desolation it changes something inside you. Desolation tries to colonize you," the biologist notes early in VanderMeer's novel. Area X's ecosystem is one that consumes the people who enter it. It is hostile and freakish: spores unravel the biologist's mind, charging boars roam the wilderness and low moans fill the night. Unlike *San Andreas* and *The Day After Tomorrow* with their overnight weather events, *Annihilation* captures just how *weird* climate change is, in all its uncanny, unpredictable, destabilising ways. Area X – like our own climate – is not an event. It has no sense of history nor of the future. It is only what we project onto it.

Against this environment, the biologist wrestles with her grief for her husband, himself lost to this uncanny labyrinth. But rather than be repulsed by Area X's freakish nature, the biologist chooses to embrace it. In *Annihilation*'s weirdest scene, the Crawler, a creature that lurks at the bottom of an inverted tower, writing on its walls with golden moss, penetrates the biologist's mind, a violation that she submits to. What if instead of fighting the climate, we let it colonise us, asks the novel. What if we let the weird in?

"We were ghosts roaming a haunted landscape, and although we didn't know it, people lived normal lives here, everything was as it should be here," writes the biologist's husband in a lost expedition diary. "But we couldn't see it through the veil, the interference." VanderMeer's Southern Reach Trilogy erases the arbitrary lines we have drawn between personal and global annihilation, instead making them one and the same. At the end of the novel, there is no boundary between human and non-human. The biologist's breakdown is the climate's breakdown.

We are already grieving for our world. The concept of climate grief – defined by ecopsychology specalist Dr. Derrick Sebree Jr. as "a depth of realisation of that recognised loss of what will never be again"[11] – looms over us as more species are made extinct, more people die and more landscapes are decimated. While climate grief seems like a modern concept, for many populations – like Indigenous communities who have had deep ties with land severed across long periods of time, from the initial colonialism of European settlers to the more recent neocolonialism of oil companies – this grief has no ending. It is an apocalypse that continues relentlessly, passed onto future generations. To grieve is a privilege; one that brings us, amongst pain, resolution and comfort. It doesn't quite have an end point – anyone who has lost a loved one can testify to that – but it does soften over time.

In her essay 'On Grief', Rebecca Tamás suggests that climate grief is not quite the right wording for what we are experiencing in regards to the climate crisis. "[A] lot of what is called 'climate grief,' is actually a kind of climate despair or melancholia," writes Tamás. "Rather than mourning for what is lost, and being galvanized to try and protect what is left, we are, understandably thrown into a darkness that makes us revolt against our very sense of being in the world."[12]

This despair described by Tamás is the melancholy that looms over many of us as we attempt to move through our lives while we simultaneously live with the awareness that we are destroying our planet. *We are collapsing into ourselves* I think as I sort plastic from paper to put in my recycling bin. *The Amazon is on fire* I think as I carry my food shopping home. *I'm going to die from climate change* I think as I sit in a park drinking a beer. *My children are going to choke and starve and drown* I think as I lower myself into a hot bath.

For the biologist in *Annihilation*, this melancholy manifests as Area X, as she folds herself into the self-destructive oblivion she finds there. Climate despair is an engulfing, impregnating oil spill. To watch the Earth collapse is to watch ourselves collapse, an annihilation that is unnatural and diabolical. It is paralysing. But in VanderMeer's novel, this desire to fold inwards offers the biologist a way out. At the end of *Annihilation*, she abandons the original mission, abandons her old world, abandons Southern Reach to go deeper into Area X, to find her husband. In this climate of despair, purpose is found.

Slavoj Žižek draws a parallel between the five stages of grief and our reckoning with our oncoming demise in his book, *Living in the End Times*. "The first reaction is one of ideological denial: there is no fundamental disorder; the second is exemplified by explosions of anger at the injustices of the new world order; the third involves attempts at bargaining [...]; when the bargaining fails, depression and withdrawal set in; finally, after passing through this zero-point, the subject no longer perceives the situation as a threat, but as the chance of a new beginning."[13]

The chance of a new beginning. In grief and despair, perhaps there is also motivation. "What occurs after revelation and paralysis?" asks the biologist at the end of *Annihilation*. Our popular cli-fi narratives – fall, redemption and resolution – should make us cautious of projecting Hollywood three-act structures onto the climate crisis, but *Annihilation* offers optimism in its ecological melancholy.

Dolphins swim down canals in Area X, having adapted to the freshwater. "They slid by," the biologist notes. "The nearest one rolled slightly to the side, and it stared at me with an eye that did not, in that brief flash, resemble a dolphin eye to me. It was painfully human, almost familiar. In an instant that glimpse was gone and they had submerged again, and I had no way to verify what I had seen."

I thought about *Annihilation*'s dolphins as I lay in bed watching doctored videos of dolphins swimming down Venice's canals, during a pandemic caused by our reckless consumption of the planet. "Nature is healing, we are the virus," read the caption. As the world collapses around us, maybe we can be forgiven for looking for hope in fictional dolphins.

Chapter 3
The Extraterrestrial Disaster

"Beam me off this planet," my thumbs type out. "Actually just knock it right out of space." Insert skull emoji.

During the first nationwide lockdown of the pandemic in early 2020, I got into a bad habit of vocalising a desire for the end of the world. Every bad news story, every slight inconvenience was met with the throwaway text: "the asteroid can't hit fast enough." The asteroid in question was, obviously, not literal but rather an emotional crux as the pandemic worsened, death tolls rose and I felt more and more useless, more and more guilty, more and more numb. A bit like muttering, "I'm going to kill myself," after reading a particularly irritating email, my request for the decimation of all life on this planet was a mechanism for self-defense and a desire for nothingness. No more news, no more doomscrolling, no more answering to loved ones. Just pure, sweet void.

The asteroid apocalypse is my favourite apocalypse. It's an especially cruel catastrophe because, unlike the climate crisis, the spread of a killer virus or zombies running rampant, it is one of very few end-of-the-world scenarios in which humans are totally innocent. It is also a nihilistic catastrophe because, sure, you could try to find a bunker, but there's no escaping something that's tearing through time and space to smash us into oblivion. You can't outrun it, outsmart it, outmanoeuvre it. Death is imminent; you might as well enjoy your final moments.

The extraterrestrial disaster can generally be divided into two subgenres: asteroid collisions and alien invasions. While space monsters have been a common threat to Earth since H.G. Wells's novel *The War of the Worlds* popularised the invasion narrative in 1897, the asteroid movie peaked in popularity more recently in the 1990s, specifically in 1998 when Michael Bay's *Armageddon* and Mimi Leder's *Deep Impact* were released within months of each other. Both films share a similar plot: a team of heroic American martyrs become Earth's last chance to save itself when a deadly space rock hurtles our way.

Armageddon, the better received and remembered of the two films, requires a team of oiler drillers to take on its asteroid. Helmed by down-to-earth, get-the-job-done

Harry, played by '90s action man Bruce Willis, the team is an all-American, all-male group of blue collar workers who scoff at NASA's pencil-pushing scientists. Saving the world is a distinctly boys' game in *Armageddon* as all the film's women are reduced to sexual objects and Harry's daughter, Grace (Liv Tyler), is little more than motivation for her dad and boyfriend to save the world – but, hey, at least they do save it.

Deep Impact, which flopped at the box office when it was released a few months before Bay's movie (although it was, at the time, the highest earning blockbuster ever directed by a woman), similarly features an ensemble cast led by journalist Jenny, played by Téa Leoni, whose boss is also a woman. The film's ensemble cast features new mothers, career women and a Black president (played by Morgan Freeman). Leder's inclusive cast was dismissed upon the film's release and *Deep Impact* was panned by *The New York Times* as "sensitive" and having a "womanly touch".[1]

Armageddon was also denounced by critics upon release for its cheesy, melodramatic tone, but Bay's film managed to capture the imagination of an audience that was living in a bubble of American exceptionalism and cowboy bravado. *Armageddon* is a vision of the world in which scientists don't know their facts from a "plastic ice cream scoop", and middle American oiler rig workers are the last hope for, not just the USA, but also the world.

Apocalypses in the 1990s were joyous and silly, appropriate for an American audience who were at relative peace in a booming economy. Hollywood disaster movies got to play with increasingly absurd *what if* scenarios – a killer hurricane! a drillable asteroid! comic murder aliens! – as audiences sat comfortably in their multiplex cinema seats, secure in America's empire.

At the turn of the century, the mood in America – and, in turn, its cultural output – changed abruptly when two airplanes hit the World Trade Centre in New York City. Scenes of disaster, previously the stuff of fantastical cinema, were broadcast live into every home in the USA, and across the world. "It's like a movie," commented news reporters over footage of smouldering buildings on live television. The country went to war and a mourning nation attempted to contend with a new narrative, one in which the USA was not impenetrable and one that made little sense to the majority of the country's citizens.

Hollywood found an audience primed to rally round a common cause, and so, disaster movies began preying on anxieties in the aftermath of 9/11. In Steven Spielberg's 2005 adaptation of *War of the Worlds*, a young girl played by Dakota Fanning cries out, "Is it the terrorists?" when the aliens arrive. *War of the Worlds* was the first major disaster movie written, shot and released post-9/11. Others that had been in production when the attack happened were either shelved or released without fanfare as, the *Los Angeles Times* reported, "the entertainment industry worries that the public appetite for plots involving disasters and terrorism has vanished."[2] Spielberg and his writers, Josh Friedman and David Koepp, needed to make their *War of the Worlds* a disaster movie for a post-9/11 audience. They chose to move away from the absurdly bombastic cinematic apocalypses of the 1990s, now considered inappropriate in this new world, and instead invoke the grim tone of a news reporter covering a catastrophe.

War of the Worlds follows downbeat father, Ray (Tom Cruise), who suddenly has to take responsibility for his estranged children (Fanning and Justin Chatwin) when aliens begin to attack Earth with tripods that can disintegrate entire populations into dust. Spielberg's *War of the Worlds* follows the episodic structure of Wells's original novel, as the family is forced to flee, first from the aliens and then from increasingly desperate, violent humans. Shots of a shell-shocked Ray coated in grey dust, people screaming and running from clouds of ash hanging over cities and a memorial wall dedicated to fallen victims are hardly subtle references to 9/11, achingly familiar to its contemporary audience.

War of the Worlds tapped into America's psychology at this time, particularly feelings of helplessness and retaliation. After Ray's son witnesses crowds of people being annihilated by the tripods, he joins a group of soldiers who are going after the aliens for revenge, screaming to his father, "We get back at them." For audiences who were still processing these emotions themselves, this desperate desire for revenge differed wildly from the male bravado of *Armageddon* and *Independence Day* (1996). And rather than the USA saving the day through human ingenuity or blowing up spaceships – a common ending to those '90s disaster movies – the aliens in *War of the Worlds* simply die because they lack immunity to Earth's airborne illnesses.

War of the Worlds ushered in a new type of disaster movie, one that attempted to invoke the horror of living through a catastrophe rather than play it for laughs. Living in a country now at war, American audiences wanted to see their lived experiences reflected back at them, and entertainment began to reflect reality as Hollywood scrambled to find stories that would respond to – and process – the horrors of living through 9/11. Although mainstream American cinema eventually returned to being more than comfortable blowing up famous national landmarks on screen again in the 2010s, *War of the Worlds* set a precedent for disaster movies honing in on individual and collective trauma. Psychological realism succeeded the grandiose, cheesy emotional arcs of '90s disaster movies. To do this, the genre moved away from ensemble casts that featured presidents and war heroes as their main characters, instead making a single family or couple their films' protagonists, as seen in *War of the Worlds*, *The Day After Tomorrow* and *The Happening* (2008).

While filmmakers were initially anxious about whether audiences would lose their appetite for fictional disaster, the hunger for these movies has only become increasingly ravenous. The extraterrestrial apocalypse has become a staple of the disaster genre. A hungry, expanding Sun threatens the Earth in Frant Gwo's 2019 blockbuster *The Wandering Earth*, while the villain of *Transformers: The Last Knight* plots to turn our world into a foreign planet. Aliens are constantly rolling up and trying to subjugate Earth: *Cloverfield*'s extraterrestrial monsters lay waste to New York; armoured spaceships wreak havoc in 2018's *Extinction*; and *A Quiet Place*'s hypersensitive-eared monsters invade from space.

But no genre has made use of space invaders quite like the modern cultural phenomenon of the superhero movie. Marvel and DC's heroes are constantly facing extraterrestrial apocalypses. In the latest Avengers movie – aptly named *Endgame* – they face an egotistical, intergalactic ecoterrorist on his quest to wipe out half of, not just Earth, but the cosmic universe, while over in the DC universe, *Justice League*'s villain tries to enslave Earth.

But, when you're constantly saving the world from total annihilation, how do you follow up with the sequel? Hollywood's superhero blockbusters have written themselves into a corner as each sequel's catastrophe needs to become progressively bigger. In Marvel's *The Avengers*, the superheroes save New York City; in the sequel, they're tasked with saving the world; in the sequel's sequel, the universe. While the disasters become visually and existentially bigger, movie audiences become increasingly numb to the stakes. Modern superhero movies suffer from a similar problem to the cli-fi genre: how can we invest in these end-of-the-world scenarios when they have become so disposable to Hollywood? In a cultural climate in which cinema has become casual about evoking images of terror on screen to an increasingly desensitised audience, the threat of mass annihilation has turned us into passive watchers. Unlike the post-9/11 sensibilities of disaster movies, like *War of the Worlds*, which sought to make the catastrophes viscerally intimate experiences, recent superhero movies have depersonalised the apocalypse. Our cinematic heroes are now deities and billionaires who bypass boring government regulations and legal logistics to blow shit up and save the day. Modern superhero films are spectacles, unquestionably fun to watch, but they exist in their own vacuums, to be consumed and then disposed of to make room for the spin-off.

Watching superhero movie after superhero movie evokes a feeling of passivity that is, sure, pleasurable: you know there's a sequel so why invest in the stakes; you know a caped crusader will show up to save the day so why care about the threat. And their popularity makes sense. In a world in which political populism reigns, the climate crisis is beyond our imagination and we're all stuck in bubbles of hysterical panic buoyed by algorithms, it's a relief to watch a movie and just – give up, to know everything will be alright in the end (except the one time in *Infinity War* when it wasn't, but then along came the sequel and… it was).

Maybe global blockbusters aren't the place to look for apocalyptic stakes, but where does that leave watching mass annihilation on our cinema screens? It's time the extraterrestrial disaster movie made the end of the world great again – or, at least, made us truly *care* about what we're watching unfold on screen. Rather than depersonalise disaster, how can cinema make us feel connected in intimate, personal ways to spectacle?

Enter: Justine.

Something is coming. It is big and blue and hanging over a wedding. So opens *Melancholia*, Lars Von Trier's 2011 film. An aquamarine planet called Melancholia is coming closer to Earth and Justine, played by Kirsten Dunst, is getting married. She and her new husband (Alexander Skarsgård) arrive late to their own reception after their stretch limousine struggles to get past bends on narrow country lanes. When they finally get to the venue, the couple is thrown into their wedding party. They dance, they play games, they converse with family and friends, including Justine's sister Claire (Charlotte

Gainsbourg). Interspersed within the party – which comprises the first act of the film – Justine leaves. She drives a golf cart across the gardens, soaks in a bathtub, crumbles into a fetal position. Justine, the film reveals, is deeply depressed. Each time she returns to the party, it is still in full swing, a seemingly never-ending fête. As Justine becomes increasingly detached from her surroundings, Von Trier allows us to creep into her head. Time warps: the party never ends, Justine sleeps, Justine leaves, Justine returns. The dancing never stops and her husband never looks for her. As the filmmaking becomes more scattershot – it shakes off characters, crash edits into different scenes and splinters time itself – Justine is left in the darkness of the party's unreal mansion, stuck floating in limbo, not unlike a planet hanging in space.

Before the wedding, *Melancholia* opens with a prologue of slow motion shots. Justine floats downstream in her wedding dress, an allusion to John Everett Millais's painting 'Ophelia'; she stands, arms spread wide, surrounded by birds in flight; her sister, Claire, sinks through the ground as she runs holding her son; the planet, Melancholia, crashes into Earth. The extreme slow motion itself evokes Justine's melancholia: the paralysis that comes from depression, the inability to move, the perverted warping of time.

After the wedding, Melancholia moves even closer to Earth. Justine's depression worsens until she is catatonic, barely able to move or speak. And then, suddenly, a switch happens. The closer Melancholia comes to hitting Earth – and the more panicked those surrounding her, particularly her sister, become – the more at peace Justine feels. She emerges from the stupor of depression, seemingly calm. Von Trier has spoken about how *Melancholia*'s apocalypse is a metaphor for depression, inspired by his own illness. While the horror of an incoming planet becomes a night marish reality for the characters surrounding Justine, she readily accepts it. "The Earth is evil," she tells Claire. Finally the chaos, the feeling of obliteration, the hopelessness, the desire for annihilation that Justine has been living with, caused by her depression, becomes material, something external and outside of her body. Now, others see it, now they understand her suffering.

When I rewatched *Melancholia* during the COVID-19 pandemic, I was struck anew by the film's portrayal of depression, the metaphor somehow deepened for me. There was Von Trier's corruption of time, a common side effect of depression when days screech to a halt or speed up to an unbearable pace. But what I noticed on my rewatch was that *Melancholia*'s apocalypse is really about a desire to be understood, to have your deepest fears and anxieties writ large upon the sky and to have the horror that only you know turned into a literal fucking planet that's coming to annihilate every person on Earth. In Von Trier's film, the extraterrestrial apocalypse doesn't bring the world together, like it commonly does in other fictional disasters. Instead, *Melancholia*'s approach to the end of the world offers something deeply intimate, a metaphorical apocalyptic spectacle that explores the intricacies of one woman's internal life.

During the pandemic, some people who suffer from mental illnesses reported that their anxiety melted away as the world seemingly caught up with them. When I asked a friend who is predisposed to sometimes daily bouts of panic attacks why she felt more at ease at the start of the pandemic, she said she was prepared, that years of battling to control her anxiety while the world carried on as normal around her, had given her an advantage now that the entire world was having a panic attack. She felt less isolated. She felt understood.

Others did not experience this sense of inner peace. Early in the pandemic, mental health severely deteriorated, particularly impacting women, young people and those with children.[3] Two-thirds of British adults reported feeling worried about the effect COVID-19 was having on their lives.[4] Childcare, job insecurity, working from home and fears of a new, unknown virus culminated in what healthcare professionals called a mental health crisis, one that will have repercussions long after the return of 'normal' life as, the UK's Centre for Mental Health estimates, at least half a million people in the UK will experience mental illnesses as a result of COVID-19.[5]

As someone with a generally apocalyptic disposition, I thought I was prepared to meet the end of days. But no movie, book or game could have primed me for the impact of lockdown on my mental health. At the start of the pandemic, I was made redundant from a new job, moved back in with my parents and waited to see if the world was going to end. I didn't have the responsibilities that many others had, but a sense of doom came to hang over me like a storm cloud. In the first few months of the pandemic my mental health plummeted. Days and weeks merged together as I struggled to get out of bed, move from room to room and go outside for my state-sanctioned daily walk. I felt a violent desire to give up and let the world move on without me – and maybe I would have if I didn't have loved ones surrounding me.

During lockdown, time played tricks. Sometimes I felt days soar past, sometimes they ground to a halt. I felt like Justine at the beginning of *Melancholia*: the world was a party and I was left behind, hanging in the dark waiting for the end.

How do we carry on when death, suffering and melancholy are inevitable in our future? The peace Justine feels at the end of the world could be described as apocalyptic desire. This desire, writes James Berger, often comprises a "combination of violent hatred for the world as it is and violent desire for the world it should be."[6] Justine watches Melancholia's trajectory towards Earth with grim pleasure. After all, as she tells Claire, the Earth is "evil". Justine's nihilism is, of course, a symptom of her depression but it also speaks to the despairing thought that haunts many of us: that maybe things would be better if we just... gave up. The climate cannot be saved so why bother trying. Humans are fundamentally evil so we shouldn't help each other. Capitalism and the impending natural disaster and every other thing we face is all encompassing and taking action is futile.

It is easy to give in to despair. Sometimes I want to give up. I want to stop giving a shit. I want to stop feeling guilty for wanting to stop giving a shit. *Melancholia* revels in this personal apocalyptic desire without moralising. The end of the world doesn't 'cure' Justine's depression; instead she chooses to meet it.

We want to give up because the future is unknowable; but disaster fiction gives us the chance to ask, would knowing our future actually change things? Denis Villeneuve's *Arrival*, released in 2016, was another extra-terrestrial disaster film I rediscovered during lockdown. *Arrival* follows Louise, a professor of comparative linguistics played by Amy Adams, who is called in to help the army when twelve monolithic spacecrafts, called heptapods, arrive on Earth.

Louise is a fascinating protagonist. Before she goes to meet the heptapods, she is profoundly alone. She works alone and lives alone but even emotionally she seems severed from the world. Flashback montages in the first half of the film reveal that Louise's daughter has died of an illness and her husband has left her. "He said I made the wrong choice," Louise tells her daughter in one flashback sequence. Her work with the heptapods takes on new significance as the bridge between Louise's grief and arriving back into the world around her.

The end of *Arrival* twists like a knife. By learning to communicate with the heptapods, Louise suddenly realises that their sense of time is unmoored from our own, their language is non-linear and therefore they see both past and future. It turns out the heptapods came to Earth because they will need our help in thousands of years' time. Louise's understanding of the alien's language allows her to visualise her own future. With a sinking heart, the film reveals that what we thought were flashbacks were in fact premonitions. Louise's unborn daughter will die in the future. She will raise her child knowing that she will lose her. She will marry her husband knowing he will leave her.

Arrival is based on Ted Chiang's short story, 'Story of Your Life' published in 1998. "What if the experience of knowing the future changed a person?" Louise asks in it. "What if it evoked a sense of urgency, a sense of obligation to act precisely as she knew she would?" *Arrival* is about choice. It is about recognising that you will experience loss, but also love, and how difficult it can be to embrace both. Louise's future is not her destiny; she can choose not to marry and not to have a child. Her husband, after all, thinks she made the wrong choice. But, despite the pain and grief and melancholy, she believes she made the right one. The good moments are worth the bad ones.

When I rewatched *Arrival* I found echoes of how I experienced time while depressed and in lockdown. In the way Louise's past and future collapse in to gently meet each other, I saw how my own chronology of living through a pandemic has warped. Sometimes I can barely remember 2020. At other times, moments are sharply realised, almost blinding. I forget entire months but then can recall every word of a phone call. I can give a compelling narrative when a stranger asks me how I coped, where I was, what I did during lockdown, but I get distracted by flashes of buried memories, the days spent under a depressive wave. I remember the joyous moments, the dinners cooked, the time spent with family – and then I abruptly forget them. I am overwhelmed by the tricks time plays on my mind. I am underwhelmed by my mind's inability to hold onto the moments that matter.

Louise's work to understand the aliens is as much about ordering events and piecing together a narrative as it is about communication. By trying to understand the extraterrestrial creatures, Louise's time is disrupted and she has to make her choice: whether or not to go into the future with what she has learned. At the end of

Arrival, the film cuts between past, present and future, squeezing them together until we're unsure which part of the narrative we're watching. The vacuum of Louise's loneliness disappears as the aliens leave behind a gift: a new way of seeing the world, one that relies on collaboration, vulnerability and choice. Unlike her husband, Louise is not devastated when she learns her future; she welcomes it in.

Although they don't have happy endings, Von Trier and Villeneuve's extraterrestrial disaster movies are far more optimistic than the false hope so often promised in superhero blockbusters. Rather than invoking the numb passivity of watching billionaires fight space aliens, Justine and Louise's apocalypses are, ironically, more down-to-earth in their recognition of the difficult decisions we have to make every day to be a person in the world.

Because we have to choose to keep going. I had to choose to climb out of my depression. Sometimes I fall back into it, sometimes I think I've left it behind forever. It's an ongoing process but one that I choose to work on. *Melancholia* and *Arrival* explore free will in apocalyptic times as their protagonists make similar choices: whether to embrace the end of the world or whether to go into the future.

Apocalyptic desire will not save us. But perhaps observing that desire in fiction, learning its shape and trying to understand why some of us yearn for it, will help us choose to pull ourselves out of it. In the ugly and difficult times we are living in, when despair can feel like a planet surging towards you, making the choice to keep going can be a painful aspiration. These extraterrestrial apocalypses offer us life rafts, not to escape from a planet on fire, but alternative ways of turning around to face our future head-on.

Chapter 4
The Social Disaster

A circle of silent women, their heads bowed. They stand in the drizzle, wearing cheap red cloaks and fraying white bonnets. Surrounded by the noise of the city, the quiet red-robed women are eerie, their uniform like a nun's habit, the colour reminiscent of a shameful scarlet letter. They stand a stone's throw away from men in police uniform. It's tense, but then one of the women breaks away. Suddenly, she's a young woman standing with her friends, head thrown back in laughter.

I saw the women – handmaids, appearing as if ripped from the pages of Margaret Atwood's seminal novel – years ago, at a rally protesting Irish abortion laws which, until the late 2010s and on both sides of the border, were some of the strictest in the world. In 2019, Northern

Ireland's theocratic legislation that made abortion a criminal offense was overruled by Westminster. Before then, those who sought abortions had to make the choice to either travel to mainland UK – a costly, sometimes traumatic journey – or administer their own abortion through pills or more medieval methods. The medical procedure was – and remains – taboo in a country where a twisted, weaponised version of Christianity continue to trip up progress. On the November day that Northern Ireland decriminalised abortion, same-sex marriage was also legalised. I watched the news roll out half a world away from my homeland. The relief and joy I felt made my hands tremble.

Growing up in Northern Ireland, before abortion was legalised, was to grow up under the crushing realisation that your body is not your own; that it is subject to the whims of a government that is largely comprised of misogynistic, religious zealots. As a teenager I watched news stories of women arrested and dragged in front of courts for taking abortion pills. I absorbed anti-abortion billboards, plastered on the sides of churches. Both north and south of the Irish border, controlling women's bodies was state-sanctioned. It was normal.

In 2012, Savita Halappanavar died in Galway after being refused an abortion. After suffering through an incomplete miscarriage, medical staff denied Halappanavar an abortion as it would have been in breach of Irish law. In that hospital, an unsavable fetus was prioritised over a 31-year-old woman's right to life. As protesters flooded the streets of Dublin and Galway over Halappanavar's death, miles away I stole a book from my school library. It was *The Handmaid's Tale*, written by the Canadian author Margaret Atwood and published in 1985. The novel is a witness account, told by an anonymous narrator, about a dystopian version of the USA called Gilead, a totalitarian country where women have lost all rights. Dehumanised to pure biological function, fertile women, known as handmaids, wear red robes and white bonnets and are forcibly assigned to bear children via state-sanctioned rape. Women who aren't handmaids are designated other roles: wives, who wear blue, oversee the home; Marthas, in green uniforms, do the cooking and cleaning; the Aunts, in muddy brown, indoctrinate the handmaids; and 'unwomen' (infertile or rebellious women) are sent away to clean toxic waste, the fallout of an environmental disaster that has caused mass infertility.

Atwood's handmaid has become a popular symbol of female protest; red-robes and white bonnets have become a common costume donned at rallies, gaining notoriety at the Women's March, organised as a response to Donald Trump's election in 2016. A year later a television adaption of *The Handmaid's Tale* premiered. "Handmaid's Tale Delivers a Timely And Feminist Message," ran an *NPR* headline, while *Syfy Wire* called the story "timeless". Atwood's novel, and the television adaption, suddenly became the go-to analogy for living as a liberal, middle-class, white woman in Trump's America and to have your rights suddenly thrown into question.

The Handmaid's Tale is not an easy television show to watch. It is often excruciatingly gruesome. Nearly every episode features scenes of women suffering from extreme violence, from rape and mutilation to mental and physical torture. Watching the show in 2017 – when the Trump administration rolled back abortion rights in the USA, and abortion was still illegal in Ireland and Northern Ireland, alongside 66 other countries[1] – I wondered if this show was meant to punish us. I was fascinated that people were watching *The Handmaid's Tale* for pleasure, as a means of escapism and entertainment.

There's something strangely satisfying about watching your worst fears play out from a safe distance. Like the desire to watch movies about pandemics during the COVID-19 outbreak, some audiences found catharsis in *The Handmaid's Tale*, particularly when it began airing during this turbulent era of American politics. Having your anxieties visualised and acknowledged in pop culture can bring an odd sense of comfort: that your deepest, individual fear also belongs to the collective zeitgeist.

The Handmaid's Tale wasn't the only dystopian story to gain popularity after Trump's inauguration. Sales of

George Orwell's *Animal Farm* and *1984* also skyrocketed after the 45th American president's election, with Penguin Random House reporting a 9,500 percent sales increase for the latter novel in 2017.[2] Sinclair Lewis's *It Can't Happen Here*, first published in 1935, reached number nine on Amazon's bestseller list after it was reissued in 2017. In turbulent times, readers look to these dystopian narratives, set in worlds that are vaguely recognisable, because they provide a framework for understanding our own political, cultural and social ecosystems. As well as reaching back to classic dystopian works, in the late 2010s a boom of new speculative fiction was published, its popularity attributed to increasingly turbulent global political situations. Sophie Mackintosh's novels *The Water Cure* (2018) and *Blue Ticket* (2020) explore strange, dystopian worlds where young women's bodies are used as bartering tools in patriarchal social orders – and both received comparisons to *The Handmaid's Tale*. *An Excess Male* (2017) by Maggie Shen King similarly interrogates fertility and bodily control.

Shen King's novel is set in an alternative future China where the nation's one child policy – a law that for decades prohibited couples from having more than one child – has caused an excess of men and a shortage of women. Arranged marriage becomes the norm and women can take up to three husbands to ensure the production of children. It might seem like this gender dynamic would grant women more power but Shen King's alternative China remains firmly patriarchal as an inequality of power simply moulds to fit the new social order. For Shen King's characters, marriage, gender and fertility are traps from which none of them can escape.

The late 2010s boom in dystopian fiction, which centres bodily autonomy and female protagonists can also be understood as a reaction against the genre itself. In fiction, women do not do well at the end of the world. Some of them die before the action even begins (*The Road*, *Light of My Life*), while the women who do make it to the apocalypse have to fight off, not just pandemics, zombies and aliens, but also rapists and murderers (*28 Days Later*, *The Walking Dead*, *Mad Max: Fury Road*). The fall of civilisation is often depicted as a 'return' to savage brutality as laws, rules and order give way to animal instinct. Cannibals and rapists roam the land and provide an additional obstacle for our heroes who must resist giving in to such depravity.

Historically, apocalypse narratives have a tendency to lean conservative. Instead of shaking up ideas of the nuclear family, patriarchal order and gendered labour, disasters in fiction often reinforce these social constructs. In the film *Light of My Life*, directed by Casey Affleck and released in 2019, a father must protect his daughter in a man's world after a pandemic wipes out the female population. The men encountered by the pair are lonely, angry and dangerous – except for, of course, Affleck's father figure who is the only good man left on Earth. Like many of the film's apocalyptic predecessors, *Light of My Life* comes to the depressing conclusion that most men will turn from law-abiding citizens into depraved rapists, child molesters and cannibals when the fictional world ends.

This common trope within the genre perpetuates a dangerous myth that sexual violence only comes from desperate circumstances and the fall of 'civilised' values – as if the performativity of living under laws protects women from violence in our real pre-apocalyptic societies. Disaster fiction often suggests that rape is only enacted by weirdo outsiders who have 'regressed' into a state of animal brutality and that women are suddenly unsafe in post-apocalyptic landscapes, as if they have never had to contend with violence before the world ended. We know that gendered violence is the result of abuses of power and inequality within established social orders. A film like *28 Days Later*, in which its female characters are nearly raped by soldiers who they thought would protect them, is a much more accurate depiction of how violence against women is perpetuated by patriarchal social orders in the world around us.

Disaster fiction is ripe for exploring social hierarchies and inequalities because the genre, with its upended world orders, can simultaneously expose and reinforce what we ordinary perceive as 'normal' social dynamics. Like sponges, post-apocalyptic narratives soak up the political and cultural zeitgeist of their moment. While *The Handmaid's Tale*'s popularity taps into anxieties around bodily autonomy sparked by Trump's presidency, films, like *It Comes At Night* (2017) and, particularly, *A Quiet Place* (2018), reflect turbulent contemporary concerns around 'traditional' family values and conservatism in an increasingly politically fractured America.

A Quiet Place stars real life couple Emily Blunt and John Krasinski (also the film's director) as Evelyn and Lee Abbott, the parents of three children, who are trying to survive a post-apocalyptic wasteland. Hulking, reptilian predators have invaded America and, although these aliens are blind and therefore unable to see their victims, their hyper-sensitive hearing has enabled them to decimate the nation's population. But, the Abbotts have a significant advantage: their daughter, Regan, is deaf, and so the family is fluent in American Sign Language, able to communicate in a world in which they are forced into silence.

A Quiet Place begins eighty-nine days into the end of the world. In the opening sequence, the family unit is attacked and the youngest son is killed after attracting the predators with a noisy toy rocket. The loss of their son turns Evelyn and Lee into apocalypse helicopter parents. They take up residence in a rural farmhouse, turning it into a fortress, stocked with surveillance equipment, traps and firearms. Barricading themselves away from the outside world, the Abbotts are free to live a somewhat ordinary existence. A heavily pregnant Evelyn occupies the domestic sphere – taking care of the children, attending to her family's needs, cooking and cleaning – while the bearded, plaid shirt-wearing Lee takes up the mantle of protector, spending his time either in the basement watching CCTV footage or venturing into the surrounding woods to scout around. The Abbotts resemble the all-American, white, nuclear family – father, mother, son and daughter – each in their designated roles.

The family's happy, isolated existence is complicated by Evelyn's pregnancy and the future prospect of a wailing, gurgling baby. In *A Quiet Place*'s silent world, a newborn is a threat to the family unit's safety, but, for Evelyn and Lee, an addition to their family unit outweighs the potential peril, affirming the family's values: that the biological, nuclear family takes priority over all else. Protecting your family against the dangerous outside world is *A Quiet Place*'s central metaphor, with Evelyn at one point whispering to her husband, "Who are we if we can't protect them?"

Upon release, amidst much of its acclaim, *A Quiet Place* was interpreted by some as a commentary on conservatism in Trump's America, labelled "regressive" by *The New York Times*[3] and "pro-life" by *The Washington Post.*[4] Although Krasinski refuted this conservative interpretation,[5] it's easy to read them into the film; especially when the plot hinges around a 'silenced' white, rural family that must close itself off from the outside world. *A Quiet Place* was the first major apocalypse film to be entirely created in the Trump era[6] and the film's politics – in that the family unit is sacred, that extending the nuclear family unit is more important than a woman's safety, that children must be protected from the dangerous outside world – taps into the very real rhetoric surrounding a return to 'simpler times' weaponised by right wing politicians.

Through the apocalypse, the Abbotts get to return to this fantasy simpler time. All day they labour: Evelyn washes clothes and farms the land while Lee strategises from his man-cave, before the family come together over dinner, joining hands and saying grace. The home is sanctity and the outside world a horrific nightmare – a comforting message when, in real life, the outside world *is* a horrific nightmare. *A Quiet Place*'s focus on the nuclear family unit, sacrificial love between parents and children and weathering the apocalypse, not through violence but by retaining familial bonds, feels like an optimistic metaphor for how to survive our turbulent political times. Rather than advocating for – or even suggesting – that there are alternative ways of living, the film reinforces the restrictive social structures that we are already all too familiar with as the foundation for human survival. And this isn't solely on Krasinski's film – far from it: disaster fiction has a long history of relying on models of social units that are overwhelmingly represented as white, suburban, heteronormative and nuclear (it infamously took *The Walking Dead* four seasons to introduce a LGBTQ+ character to its zombie apocalypse). The social, political and economic systems that we have internalised as normal (see also: capitalism, individualism, patriarchal gender roles) have an amazing ability to survive even the apocalypse. But, where does that leave those who don't fit comfortably into what the genre has reinforced as 'normative' social models? What place do they have at the end of the world?

In the hands of women and people of colour, disaster narratives more often become tools to interrogate pre-existing sexist and racist social systems. In Octavia Butler's *Parable* novel series, beginning with *Parable of the Sower* in 1993, a young Black woman called Lauren lives in an alternative "oozing sore" fictional version of Los Angeles. Set in 2024, *Parable of the Sower* presents a world that is more similar than dissimilar to our own: late capitalism, mass incarceration and social decay, exacerbated by climate change, has resulted in an enormous gap of wealth inequality. While a failing president spouts his slogan, "make America great again" (nearly 25 years before that phrase found its way onto Trump's red hats), Lauren and her middle class equivalent family live in a gated community which protects them from the violence of those living beyond its walls in abject poverty. After the community is broken into, Lauren, dressed as a man, escapes with a few of her surviving neighbours to head north, joining a stream of refugees desperately fleeing the freak weather, rampant racism and murderous bandits.

On this journey, Lauren creates her own religion based on her abilities as a 'hyperempath', a psychological condition which forces her to experience the emotions of those surrounding her. As the leader of her group, Lauren must cautiously decide whether or not to let others join them and soon an extended chosen family unit forms, one that is made up of the most vulnerable people in *Parable of the Sower*'s world: mixed race couples, new mothers and young women. Lauren's group survives through their collective action which was inspired by the politics of '60s Black Power and Black feminist groups. Butler presents her vision of a new social order: one that is led by a young, empathetic Black woman and one that holds respect for others, mutual aid and collaboration at its core.

Butler's *Parable* series demonstrates that if we continue down a path of rampant capitalism and unsustainable environmental destruction, our future will not be worth living for, as Lauren's society disintegrates around her and she continually loses loved ones to the novel's hellish nightmare version of Los Angeles. Rather than shutting herself off from the deadly outside world, Lauren is forced to confront it through her hyperempathy with no option of detaching from the people around her, even those who wish her and her group harm. *Parable of the Sower* presents this forced connectivity as the way in which we start to build a better future for ourselves, especially when our society, politics and economic structures want to keep us isolated. Lauren, and Butler, reject pessimistic fatalism and instead see the crumbling world around us as an opportunity to rebuild something better. When you're already in hell, burn it down and start again.

Optimism in dire circumstances also drives *Children of Men*, the 2006 film directed by Alfonso Cuarón, adapted from P. D. James's 1992 novel of the same name. *Children of Men*'s world is one that is running out of time. At the start of the film it has been 18 years since a child has been born, and mass infertility – coupled with waves of asylum seekers, the result of ongoing global warfare – has left mankind on the brink of collapse. The story's main character, a bureaucrat named Theo (played by Clive Owen), is tasked with protecting a refugee woman, Kee (Clare-Hope Ashitey), who is miraculously pregnant and being transported to safety by an activist group. Theo is a perfect stand-in for Friedrich Nietzsche's concept of western civilisation's 'Last Man', which Slavoj Žižek expands upon as "an apathetic creature with no great passion or commitment. Unable to dream, tired of life."[7]

The 'Last Man' protagonist has become disaster fiction's favourite trope. Always a man – and usually a white one – he is a rugged, emotionally repressed survivor. He is Joe in *The Last of Us*, Rick in *The Walking Dead*, Robert in Richard Matheson's 1954 novel *I am Legend*, and the protagonist of Mary Shelley's 1826 novel aptly titled *The Last Man*. The character is an impressive survivor, able to fight off whichever supernatural monsters have caused his apocalypse, skilled, strong and resilient. And the popularity of this apocalyptic trope has had resounding real life implications, most notably in the rise of the doomsday prepper. Like the 'Last Man', doomsday preppers are almost exclusively white American men who believe they need to be ready for a future disaster, whether it's man-made, natural or extraterrestrial. Prepping as a lifestyle involves hoarding vast quantities of kit and supplies, building bunkers far away from urban populations and training to survive whichever disaster comes first. On the internet, prepping as a subculture is presented as one about resilience, self-sufficiency and resourcefulness. Bearded men in baseball caps and flannel shirts display their kits for when it will be time to 'bug out' – in other words, when shit gets real and it's time to hit the bunker. These 'hauls', in which knives, ropes and dehydrated meat are laid out, are accompanied with giddy excitement from their owners.

For these preppers, future disasters are a test of their masculinity. They need to be as strong as Dwayne Johnson hanging from a helicopter in *San Andreas*, or as resilient as John Krasinski sprinting through the woods in *A Quiet Place*, or as resourceful as Bruce Willis blowing up an asteroid in *Armageddon*. The end of the world isn't what's important to preppers – in fact, many of them seem to relish the prospect. What *is* important to them is buying the right kit, gaining the right skills and having the right kind of mentality to beat the end of the world. Surviving is very much a Social-Darwinist competition.

In disaster fiction, the character arc of the 'Last Man' usually involves him reconnecting with other survivors, opening up and regaining a sense of lost humanity, an aspect to Johnson, Krasinski and Willis's characters' narratives that doomsday preppers tend to ignore. *Children of Men*'s Theo, is one who is caught in between a state of despair and a new-found motivation sparked by the discovery of Kee. A man with nothing to live for, Theo is suddenly emboldened to take action to prevent humanity's extinction. By the end of the film, an alternative future is possible with the birth of Kee's baby, a world that is presented as having no more space for Theo's 'Last Man'. This western ideal quite literally dies at the end of the film, and Kee instead takes Theo's place. Like in *Parable of the Sower*, Cuarón's film proposes that if we don't act now, we are on a trajectory to becoming the 'Last

Men' of the Global North: exploitative, desensitised and too far gone in our despair to even hope for a different future. Cuarón has to kill off the trope in order to present an alternative future to the archetypal survivor we so often romanticise in disaster fiction. In fact, *Children of Men* suggests that our only hope for survival is to leave the 'Last Man' behind. It is Kee, a Black refugee woman, who will pave our way into the future.

No one apocalypse is universal. What is perceived as the end of the world for the disaster fiction's characteristic leading man and doomsday preppers can be, simultaneously, the beginning of a new, more hopeful world for those who have been historically oppressed. What is total social collapse for one person, is a revolution for someone else. Controlling populations can be a utopia for the ruling minority, but a dystopia for the oppressed majority. Rather than a fixed moment in time, the apocalypse is constantly in flux, beginning and ending and beginning and ending over and over and over again.

For middle class, liberal feminists in 2016, *The Handmaid's Tale* suddenly became a possibility, while numerous Black and migrant women have already experienced forced sterilisation and abortions in the USA. For the Global North, cli-fi movies are pure escapism, while in the Global South, freak weather, tsunamis and earthquakes are already a regular occurrence creating thousands of climate refugees. For *Children of Men*'s

Theo, the world is not worth living for, while for Kee, only now that old social orders are collapsing, is it *finally* worth living for.

At the beginning of the COVID-19 pandemic, healthcare organisations and politicians told us that "this virus does not discriminate."[8] But it soon became horrifyingly clear that the structures of our societies turned a virus into an apocalypse that did, in fact, discriminate. The intersecting inequalities of poverty and racism resulted in Black and Asian people dying from COVID-19 at twice the rate of white people in the UK.[9] Those who worked frontline jobs – not just healthcare workers, but also supermarket staff, delivery drivers and transit workers – were put at risk while those with white collar office jobs could barricade themselves at home, relying on the labour of those most at risk to provide them with food and services.

Real world disasters can have terrible consequences, but the disasters themselves rarely cause societal problems in isolation; instead they simply exacerbate inevitably catastrophic, long-held political, cultural and economic systems. As we begin to live a post-apocalyptic life following a global pandemic, we need to decide whether we are going to use this latest catastrophe to propose alternative, more sustainable and fair models to overhaul our inept social orders – or fall back on what we have always done before. Do we want to live clinging on to past structures that have failed us or, like *Children of Men*'s Kee and *Parable of the Sower*'s Lauren, do we want to find alternative ways to move into the future?

Disaster fiction gives us the space to explore radical and hopeful futures that often follow on from dystopian societies that contain more than a few similarities to our own world. Our collective dilemma shouldn't be who do we have to sacrifice to survive disaster, but instead, how do we move forward into a fairer future without leaving anyone behind.

Conclusion
After the Blast

Where do you go after you've been to the end of the world?

This is the question I asked myself as I watched disaster movie after disaster movie and read dystopian novel after dystopian novel in the process of writing *The End*. These fictional stories would only take me so far through the apocalypse and then – they stopped. Whatever happens to our protagonists after the closing credits? Do new societies form from the ashes of broken ones? What do these fictional worlds look like in ten, twenty, a hundred years? Even that childhood dream that haunted my nights for years; I would step on a crack and wake up as a nuclear explosion went off. But what happens when the mushroom cloud dissipates? What does the world look like after the blast?

As I watched films about pandemics killing millions while, outside my door, a pandemic killed millions, I wanted more from these fictional apocalypses. I wanted a blueprint plan for our future, a guide to take us into the unknown that looms ahead.

Or that's what I thought I wanted.

Now, I realise that I hadn't solely turned to fictional disasters to try to get a sneak preview into an uncharted future. What I was truly seeking from all these apocalyptic stories was something more simple: space and time. Specifically, a space in which time stops and I could dwell and process the emotions of the last day, week or year. By playing a video game or reading a novel or watching a film, you receive a limited time frame, an arc, a satisfying conclusion. Time compresses to fit art's structures. And when time slows down, it makes patterns and correlations apparent: a zombie movie can speak to rampant globalisation; a cli-fi novel can capture the horror of living during the climate crisis; an asteroid can be a metaphor for depression; a dystopian society can reflect our worst tendencies back to us like a funhouse mirror. And it can do so in a way that doesn't consume our whole life but instead packages it neatly into something easier to contend with. It can also – dare I say – bring some much needed enjoyment into the world-ending equation.

We are living in disastrous times. This is not a new phenomenon – has there ever been a time in human history not plagued with disaster? – but that knowledge doesn't make living right now any easier. The apocalypse has infiltrated our politics, economics, social structures, technologies, workplaces and homes. Scrolling through my Twitter timeline, an act that can be more adequately described as doomscrolling, I am bombarded by disaster after disaster: another irreversible climate catastrophe, abortion rights rolled back, another wave of a virus, deadly explosions, a racist attack, wildfires, a company sacking hundreds of employees, the worst recession since the last worst recession, a friend of a friend's sister dying on a ventilator, a country's healthcare sold to a private firm owned by a billionaire, space trash orbiting our planet, a city falling into the hands of dictators. Each disastrous moment so singularly terrible, it's impossible to take any of them in.

So, when life outside our windows is so unbearable, why do we turn to disaster fiction? Why do we spend our finite time with a post-apocalyptic video game, a book set in a decimated landscape forty years into the future or a television show about violent dystopian societies, to escape from our own real world version? Why don't we abandon disaster in search of its utopian opposite?

The apocalypse is a wonderfully malleable narrative device. It can be existential or literal – and usually it is both, simultaneously. It can take all the anxieties of a moment and disseminate them into plot, narrative, character and theme. A post-9/11 adaption of *The War of the Worlds* can encompass the terror and animosity of the USA in the early 2000s, while an eco-disaster novel like *Annihilation* can present climate despair as both an individual's and a landscape's grief. Disaster fiction makes terrible prospects manageable. It locates our collective culture's greatest fears and puts them at arm's length – on a screen, in a book – and let's us project, probe and pull at their unwieldy shapes. It's why so many of us sought out pandemic stories during a real pandemic. Maybe for some it was simply distraction, maybe for others it was to glimpse ahead into the future, to try and see where this real pandemic could go – but I think for most it was because fiction, with its structures, expositions and endings, give us the focus we crave from a world that is so unwieldy, so staggering, so crushing, a world fit to burst at the seams.

Apokálypsis. To uncover, to reveal. In 2020, I kept coming back to this definition of the apocalypse. What have we learned from our most recent real world catastrophes: a global pandemic, late capitalism, Big Data, the climate crisis? Looking at the big picture, it seems not much. Governments continue to cut welfare funding, corporations continue to make millions at the expense of workers' safety and billionaires are more interested in shooting off into space than protecting our finite natural resources. It is easy to be overwhelmed with apocalyptic despair. Wanting to throw in the towel is a rational response to the unending wheel of disaster that is grinding us all down. It's no wonder that we love disaster fiction so much: surely the world ending and starting again is better than whatever *this* is?

But then I look at the smaller details of that bigger, sprawling picture. I see mutual aid groups springing up to take care of their local communities. I see radical environmentalists who refuse to bow down to pressure from oil companies. I see grassroots activists rising up to fight social injustices. While 2020 saw the COVID-19 pandemic exacerbate economic inequalities, it also saw the Black Lives Matter and Stop Asian Hate movements surge forward to say, *enough is enough; we have the right to decide our own future*.

In her book, *A Paradise Built in Hell*, Rebecca Solnit writes: "Horrible in itself, disaster is sometimes a door back into paradise, the paradise at least in which we are who we hope to be, do the work we desire, and are each our sister's and brother's keeper." If disaster fiction teaches us anything, it's that there are always survivors. And those survivors get to remake society for better or worse. These apocalyptic stories can be read as cautionary tales for where our world is going, or as the foundations for imagining a better future.

When I think of disaster fiction, I don't think of the selfish, violent, regressed antagonists. I think of characters like *Severance*'s Candace, or *Annihilation*'s biologist, or *Arrival*'s Louise, or *The Handmaid's Tale*'s unnamed narrator, or *Parable of the Sower*'s Lauren, or *Children of Men*'s Kee. I think of characters who refuse to just survive, but who live because they find purpose at the end of the world. And without purpose we may as well give in to despair.

The first time the world ended, I was six years old. It has ended hundreds of times since then. True to its original meaning, the apocalypse reveals both the best and the worst of what we already have and who we already are. Disaster fiction can help us imagine new, alternative, brighter ways of living. These stories can be doors into paradise. If we turn the handle and crack them open, if we let the light in and step across the threshold, who knows what our future could hold.

References

Introduction

1. "It's Always the End of the World as We Know It." Denis Dutton, *The New York Times*, 31 December 2009. www.nytimes.com/2010/01/01/opinion/01dutton.html. Accessed 7 September 2021.
2. "From Freaked to Fine: Celebs React to Y2K (1999) | MTV News." *YouTube*, uploaded by MTV News, 23 December 2019. www.youtube.com/watch?v=x65AAsVNxKI. Accessed 7 September 2021.
3. "One in seven thinks end of world is coming: poll." Chis Michaud, Reuters, 1 May 2012. www.reuters.com/article/us-mayancalendar-poll-idUSBRE8400XH20120501. Accessed 7 September 2021.
4. "Beyond 2012: Why the World Didn't End." *NASA,* 22 December 2021. www.nasa.gov/topics/earth/features/2012.html. Accessed 7 September 2021.
5. "Review of the economy in 2012: This was not supposed to happen." Ben Chu, *Independent*, 22 December 2012. www.independent.co.uk/news/business/analysis-and-features/review-economy-2012-was-not-supposed-happen-8424651.html. Accessed 7 September 2021.

Chapter 1: The Pandemic Disaster

1. "Contagion becomes one of the most-watched films online in wake of coronavirus pandemic." Jacob Stolworthy, *Independent*, 15 March 2020. www.independent.co.uk/arts-entertain-

ment/films/news/contagion-coronavirus-download-watch-online-otorrent-warner-bros-cast-twitter-a9403256.html. Accessed 7 September 2021.

2. "Race Hate Crimes Against East And Southeast Asian People Have Quadrupled In Wake Of Coronavirus." Peter Yeung, *Huffington Post*, 21 May 2020. www.huffingtonpost.co.uk/entry/racist-hate-crime-asian-communities-quadruples-coronavirus_uk_5ec53356c5b6d5f53f85f4f1. Accessed 7 September 2021.
3. "UK suffers biggest drop in economic output in 300 years." Valentina Romei, *Financial Times*, 12 February 2021. www.ft.com/content/96e19afd-88b3-4e8d-bc3e-a72bd1f60d3c. Accessed 7 September 2021.
4. "The UK's Covid-19 unemployment crisis in six charts." Richard Partington, *The Guardian*, 3 February 2021. www.theguardian.com/business/2021/feb/03/the-uks-covid-19-unemployment-crisis-in-six-charts. Accessed 7 September 2021.
5. "Jeff Bezos became even richer thanks to Covid-19. But he still won't protect Amazon workers." Robert Reich, *The Guardian*, 13 December 2020. www.theguardian.com/commentisfree/2020/dec/12/jeff-bezos-amazon-workers-covid-19-scrooge-capitalism. Accessed 7 September 2021.
6. "Campaigners warn that 9 out of 10 people in poor countries are set to miss out on COVID-19 vaccine next year." *Oxfam*, 9 December 2020. www.oxfam.org/en/press-releases/campaigners-warn-9-out-10-people-poor-countries-are-set-miss-out-covid-19-vaccine. Accessed 7 September 2021.
7. "Zombies and the End of Society." James Berger, *E-International Relations*, 15 February 2013. www.e-ir.info/2013/02/15/zombies-and-the-end-of-society/. Accessed 7 September 2021.

Chapter 2: The Climate Disaster

1. "Australia's fires 'killed or harmed three billion animals'." *BBC News*, 28 July 2020. www.bbc.co.uk/news/world-australia-53549936. Accessed 7 September 2021.

2. “Britain’s weather office issues its first-ever extreme heat warning.” Kaly Soto, *The New York Times*, 19 July 2021. https://www.nytimes.com/2021/07/19/us/uk-heat-wave.html. Accessed 7 September 2021.
3. “Humanity is waging war on nature, says UN secretary general.” Fiona Harvey, *The Guardian*, 2 December 2020. www.theguardian.com/environment/2020/dec/02/humanity-is-waging-war-on-nature-says-un-secretary-general-antonio-guterres. Accessed 7 September 2021.
4. Ibid.
5. “7M people died of hunger in 2020, World Food Programme says.” *Daily Sabah*, 13 October 2020. www.dailysabah.com/world/7m-people-died-of-hunger-in-2020-world-food-programme-says/news. Accessed 7 September 2021.
6. “Concern about climate change reaches record levels with half now ‘very concerned’” Gideon Skinner, *Ipsos MORI*, 12 August 2019. www.ipsos.com/ipsos-mori/en-uk/concern-about-climate-change-reaches-record-levels-half-now-very-concerned. Accessed 7 September 2021.
7. Sontag, Susan. ‘The Imagination of Disaster.’ *Against Interpretation and Other Essays*. Penguin Classics, 2009.
8. “The Arctic is in a death spiral. How much longer will it exist?” Gloria Dickie, *The Guardian*, 13 October 2020. www.theguardian.com/us-news/ng-interactive/2020/oct/13/arctic-ice-melting-climate-change-global-warming. Accessed 7 September 2021.
9. Ghosh, Amitav. *The Great Derangement: Climate Change and the Unthinkable*. University of Chicago Press, 2016.
10. “Annihilation, Utopia, and Climate Change.” *The Atlantic*, 7 May 2018. www.theatlantic.com/video/index/559790/jeff-vandermeer/. Accessed 7 September 2021.
11. “‘Climate Grief’ Explained, And How To Cope With It.” Nylah Burton, *Vogue*, 10 October 2020. www.vogue.co.uk/arts-and-lifestyle/article/climate-grief. Accessed 7 September 2021.
12. Tamás, Rebecca. ‘On Grief.’ *Strangers: Essays on the Human and Nonhuman*. Makina Books, 2020.
13. Žižek, Slavoj. *Living in the End Times*. Verso Books, 2011.

Chapter 3:
The Extraterrestrial Disaster

1. "FILM REVIEW; How Do You Reroute A Comet? Carefully." Janet Maslin, *The New York Times*, 8 May 1998. www.nytimes.com/1998/05/08/movies/film-review-how-do-you-reroute-a-comet-carefully.html. Accessed 7 September 2021.
2. "Hollywood Executives Rethink What Is Off Limits." Claudia Eller, *Los Angeles Times*, 14 September 2001. www.latimes.com/archives/la-xpm-2001-sep-14-mn-45730-story.html. Accessed 7 September 2021.
3. Pierce, Matthias; Hope, Holly; Ford, Prof Tasmin; Hatch, Prof Stephani; Hotopf, Prof Matthew; John, Prof Ann. (2020). "Mental health before and during the COVID-19 pandemic: a longitudinal probability sample survey of the UK population." *The Lancet*, Vol. 7, No. 10, p. 883-892. doi.org/10.1016/S2215-0366(20)30308-4
4. "Emerging evidence on COVID-19's impact on mental health and health inequalities." Louise Marshall, Jo Bibby, Isabel Abbs, *The Health Foundation*, 18 June 2020. www.health.org.uk/news-and-comment/blogs/emerging-evidence-on-covid-19s-impact-on-mental-health-and-health. Accessed 7 September 2021.
5. "At least half a million more people in UK may experience mental ill health as a result of Covid-19, says first forecast from Centre for Mental Health." *Centre for Mental Health*, 15 May 2020. www.centreformentalhealth.org.uk/news/least-half-million-more-people-uk-may-experience-mental-ill-health-result-covid-19-says-first-forecast-centre-mental-health. Accessed 7 September 2021.
6. Berger, James. *After the End: Representations of Post-apocalypse*. University of Minnesota Press, 1999.

Chapter 4:
The Social Disaster

1. "The World's Abortion Laws." *Center for Reproductive Rights*, maps.reproductiverights.org/worldabortionlaws?cate-

gory[294]=294. Accessed 7 September 2021.
2. "The Real Reason Dystopian Fiction Is Roaring Back." Charley Locke, *Wired*, 22 February 2017. www.wired.com/2017/02/dystopian-fiction-why-we-read/. Accessed 7 September 2021.
3. "The Silently Regressive Politics of "A Quiet Place"." Richard Brody, *The New Yorker*, 10 April 2018. www.newyorker.com/culture/richard-brody/the-silently-regressive-politics-of-a-quiet-place. Accessed 7 September 2021.
4. "Opinion: 'A Quiet Place' isn't just pro-life. It makes us understand what being pro-life truly means." Sonny Bunch, *The Washington Post*. www.washingtonpost.com/gdpr-consent/?next_url=https%3a%2f%2fwww.washingtonpost.com%2fnews%2fact-four%2fwp%2f2018%2f04%2f11%2fa-quiet-place-isnt-just-pro-life-it-makes-us-understand-what-being-pro-life-truly-means%2f. Accessed 7 September 2021.
5. "John Krasinski Doesn't Agree With The Conservative Read on A Quiet Place." Christopher Rosen, *Vanity Fair,* 20 February 2020. www.vanityfair.com/hollywood/2020/02/john-krasinski-politics-conservative-quiet-place. Accessed 7 September 2021.
6. "Why A Quiet Place is the apocalyptic movie America needed." Aja Romano, *Vox,* 14 May 2018. www.vox.com/culture/2018/4/27/17275544/a-quiet-place-family-drama-apocalypse-politics. Accessed 7 September 2021.
7. Žižek, Slavoj. *Violence: Six sideways reflections*. Profile Books, 2008.
8. "Coronavirus: 'Virus does not discriminate' - Gove." *Sky News,* 27 March 2020. news.sky.com/video/coronavirus-virus-does-not-discriminate-gove-11964771. Accessed 7 September 2021.
9. "Why have Black and South Asian people been hit hardest by COVID-19?" *Office for National Statistics,* 14 December 2020. www.ons.gov.uk/peoplepopulationandcommunity/healthandsocialcare/conditionsanddiseases/articles/whyhaveblackandsouthasianpeoplebeenhithardestbycovid19/2020-12-14. Accessed 7 September 2021.

Acknowledgements

Firstly, thank you to the filmmakers, game designers and novelists who make the art which makes the end of the world a little more bearable.

This book began life in many different ways and in many different places. One of them was in a feature for *The Skinny* published in January, 2020. My thanks to the magazine and its editor Rosamund West for the space to begin writing about the end of the world.

Thank you Heather McDaid and Laura Jones at 404 Ink for publishing this book and for your guidance, expertise and patience. And thank you Luke Bird for the apocalyptic cover design (a compliment, I promise!).

Many people supported this book, whether they know it or not, though conversations, WhatsApp voicenotes or by picking up the phone. A special thank you to: Katie Hawthorne, Rhona Kappler, Tara Shields, Lizzy Olliver,

Harry Harris, Rachel Arthur, Ali Campbell, Anahit Behrooz and Josie Maltinsky Gaitens. Thank you Riyoko Shibe for sharing a desk with me, for reading that first draft and for being the only person to ask for an acknowledgment. Couldn't have done it without you, dude.

This book is dedicated to my grandparents, my four pillars: Audrey and Sam Alexander, Ang Wei Lan 翁惠兰 and Goh Cheng Leong 吴祯隆. Thank you to them and to my family on both sides of the world. Thank you to my brothers, Darrell and Callum Goh. Thank you to my parents, Merle and Tuck Goh. None of this would have been possible without your love, care and support.

About the Author

Katie Goh is a writer, critic and editor. She covers culture for publications like *i-D*, *VICE*, *Huck*, *the Guardian* and *gal-dem*, and is the Intersections Editor for *The Skinny*. In 2019, Katie was shortlisted for PPA Scotland's Young Journalist of the Year award and in 2021 she was invited to join the UK Film Critics' Circle. She lives in Edinburgh. Twitter: @johnnys_panic.

About the Inklings series

This book is part of 404 Ink's Inkling series which presents big ideas in pocket-sized books.
They are all available at 404ink.com/shop

If you enjoyed this book, you may also enjoy these titles in the series:

On His Royal Badness: The Life and Legacy of Prince's Fashion – Casci Ritchie

On His Royal Badness examines how Prince's distinctive style both on and beyond the screen disrupts hegemonic, heteronormative and Black masculinities and contemporary fashion more generally. Taking core pieces from his wardrobe, Ritchie embarks on a wide-ranging exploration of how the simplest of pieces can tell the most incredible of stories.

Flip The Script: How Women Came to Rule Hip Hop – Arusa Qureshi

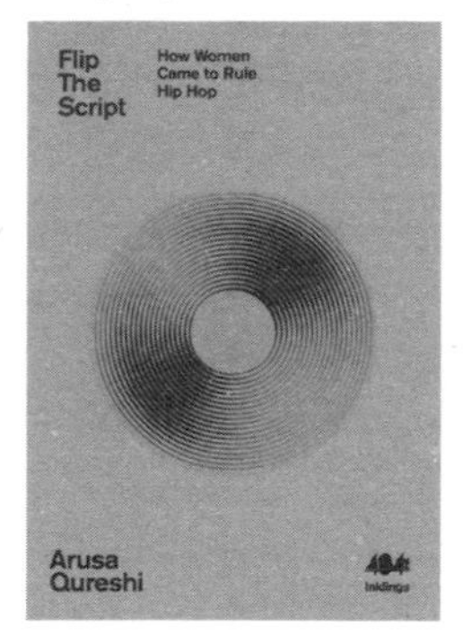

Flip The Script showcases some of the best rappers currently making music in the UK. It has taken ages for women to get the recognition they deserve in the genre, despite its beginnings in the Bronx in the 1970s – why did we take so long in the UK? *Flip The Script* gets to know the women who have paved the way, the successes and experiences of those that shape the thriving scene we have today.

Love That Journey For Me: The Queer Revolution of *Schitt's Creek* – Emily Garside

Love That Journey For Me dives deep into the cultural sensation of Canadian comedy-drama *Schitt's Creek*. Considering the fusion of existing sitcom traditions, references and tropes, this Inkling analyses the nuance of the show and its surrounding cultural and societal impact as a queer revolution.